THE IMPERATIVE OF RESPONSE

The Holocaust in Human Context

Robert Seitz Frey
Nancy Thompson-Frey

UNIVERSITY
PRESS OF
AMERICA

LANHAM • NEW YORK • LONDON

Copyright © 1985 by

University Press of America,® Inc.

4720 Boston Way
Lanham, MD 20706

3 Henrietta Street
London WC2E 8LU England

All rights reserved
Printed in the United States of America

Library of Congress Cataloging in Publication Data

Frey, Robert Seitz, 1955-
 The imperative of response.

   Bibliography: p.
   1. Holocaust, Jewish (1939-1945)—Moral and ethical
 aspects. 2. Holocaust (Christian theology) 3. Holocaust
 (Jewish theology) 4. Frey, Robert Seitz, 1955-   .
 5. Thompson-Frey, Nancy, 1955-   . 6. Proselytes
 and proselyting, Jewish—Biography. I. Thompson-Frey,
 Nancy, 1955-   . II. Title.
 D810.J4F7335 1985   940.53'15'03924   85-5324
 ISBN 0-8191-4633-1 (alk. paper)
 ISBN 0-8191-4634-X (pbk. : alk. paper)

All University Press of America books are produced on acid-free
paper which exceeds the minimum standards set by the National
Historical Publications and Records Commission.

To

Rivka Annette Frey

our daughter, our delight

and

Joshua Seitz Frey

our son

who was born October 17, 1984

and died January 13, 1985

I believe life to be of such nature that human greatness, goodness, and pinnacles of feeling and love exist untainted but for a short moment of time. Like the crest of an ocean wave, and the tiny droplets of spray that issue forth from it, so are human moments of unencumbered happiness and fullness of spirit. Most quickly, however, these moments, as with saline spray of the ocean, are subsumed by the abiding resonance of the mundane. The weight and volume of daily existence upswell to reabsorb the pristine warmth and beauty of what can be. Perhaps it suffices to know that what can be indeed is.

R.S.F.

The universe whispers that all things are intertwined. Yet at times we hear the loud cry of discord. To which voice shall we listen? Although we long for harmony, we cannot close our ears to the noise of war, the rasp of hate. How dare we speak of concord, when the fact and symbol of our age is Auschwitz?

<u>Gates of Prayer</u>

CONTENTS

		Page
	Foreword.	xi
	Preface.	xv
	Acknowledgments.	xvii
	Introduction.	xix
I	The Relevance of the Holocaust for Human Reflection.	1
II	The Holocaust as It Might Affect Christian Theology.	19
III	The Holocaust and My Conversion to Judaism.	56
IV	Some Jewish Perspectives on HaShoah.	75
V	The Holocaust, Scientific Rationality, and Transcendence: Critique and Synthesis.	87
VI	Specific Pathways of Response to the Holocaust.	121
VII	The Holocaust Reconsidered.	140
	Bibliography.	144
	About the Authors.	165

illustration

The Imperative of Response

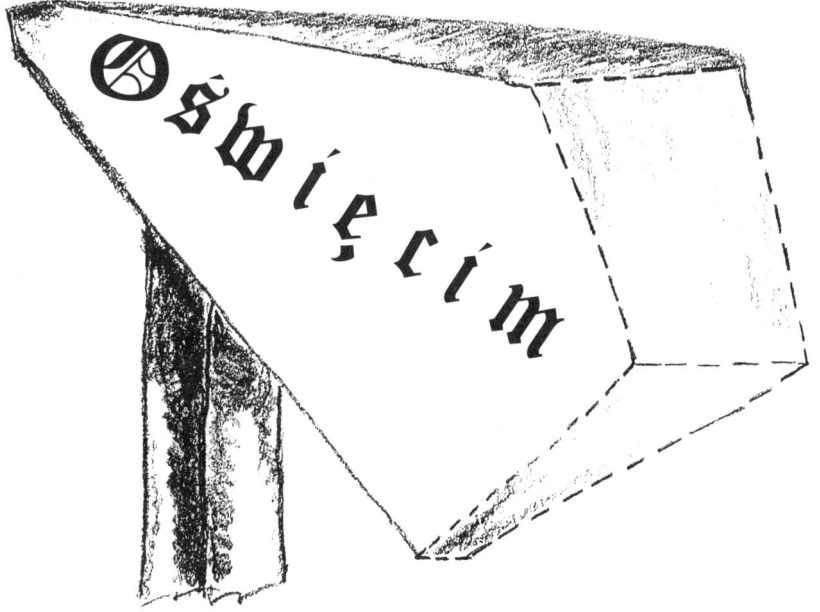

ROBERT SEITZ FREY
and
NANCY THOMPSON-FREY

FOREWORD

by

Harry James Cargas

Autobiography is a form whereby a person may seek to either discover a life or to express it. The author seems to ask and to attempt to respond to questions about the meaning of life "and my place in it." In his great confession, Augustine saw that it was the gift of his faith which put his life in its proper context. He had a vision, it marked him for life, and he experienced what a poet some fifteen centuries later was to label "The Hound of Heaven" from which Francis Thompson had no escape. Without denying the concept of free will, there seemed a certain inevitability to Augustine's story.

But if Augustine's vision was almost instantaneous, Dante's "Life of faith" evolved through a series of experiences as he details them in La Vita Nuova. The concept of faith, of the action of God through the individual human being, is essential in both works. There is a change, however, in the story of John Bunyan's life, Grace Abounding where the accent is on the individual. William Spengemann has characterized this first major Protestant autobiography as a "how to" book which is itself a present action, part of the life being described.

This somehow leads away from the Augustinian avowal that the doctrines of faith are without, not within as Bunyan implies if not downright avers. This is but a step then to the secularized view of life found in a volume like The Autobiography of Benjamin Franklin with its emphasis not on revelation but on self-reliance. Franklin's is, of course, a genuinely polemic "how to" production cum rationale. Next we might mention Rousseau who felt that he was born not to find faith, as it were, but to lose it. The natural purity of his soul had been soiled by a sinful society. He celebrated his uniqueness both as a personality and in his Confessions which led one of his admirers, Johann Wolfgang von Goethe to write of the formation of a particular personality in all of its uniqueness, with grace and style, in one of the greatest of all autobiographies.

More recent examples of the genre of self-revelation, self-discovery, apologia or other types are better known to contemporary readers. There are many students of the form who recognize in poetic, fiction and dramatic modes the embodiment of autobiography even where "facts" are absent, symbolically present or even deliberately misleading.

However, the autobiographies of Holocaust survivors have introduced certain original elements into the ever metamorphosing shape of the genre. One particularly novel aspect is the illustration of faith in spite of God's actions, or perhaps more precisely, God's inactivity. |Many Jews have accused God of breaking the covenant made with the Jewish people by failing to rescue them at Auschwitz, Buchenwald, Treblinka, Dora, Bergen-Belsen, Sobibor, Majdanek, Mauthausen, Vilna, Ponary, Chelmo, Ohrdruf, the Warsaw Ghetto... The list is agonizingly long. And yet, perhaps surprisingly to some of lesser spirituality, faith in God was not diminished for many of the victims. Trust may have been lost, but not faith. And in some cases renewed faith developed.

(Later were to come the encounters with faith described by Solzhenitsyn in the Gulag, by Cleaver in his Soul on Ice, by Mihajlo Mihajlov in Underground Notes, Kim Chi Ha in Korea and so many others. The subgenre of prison spiritual autobiographies -- of which Bunyan's is one, slave narratives are others -- is deserving of special study.)

We have accounts of Jewish learned men putting God on trial in concentration camps. Some found the Creator of the universe guilty of apathy toward the Chosen People. Others concluded that what they were experiencing was the birth pangs of the coming of the Messiah. What faith each of these positions illustrates.

Robert Frey contributes another dimension in the autobiography of religious experience. I see this book as an autobiography with commentary. In what follows he tells us of his step in faith as a response to the Auschwitz event of which he had no direct part. But as a person born Christian, he deliberately assumes the past of his people. His conclusion, which he humbly does not hold up as a model for others, is in an adjectival sense, truly christian. As Frey has observed, here,| "Christian involvement in and silence to the mass murder of Jews, the very people from whom is derived theological perspective and spiritual sustenance, strikes at a basic level -- as son to father." Indeed, "as son to father." His own re-commitment, as it were, to Judaism, in addition to being the very true act that it is, has post-Holocaust symbolic significance as well. Frey's move into Judaism can be seen as one of atonement, paralleling the act of at-one-ment of Jesus with his heavenly father.

Frey's realization of his spirituality came not in the flash of a Paul or an Augustine but rather through contemplation of the awesome Event of the 6,000,000 deaths. Camus has written that he who is not with the victims is with the executioners. Elie Wiesel has said the same thing. So have such different authors as Alexander Solzhenitsyn, Carlos Fuentes, Viktor Frankl, Takis Sinopoulus, Herman Hesse, Edward Kuznetsov and others. Frey understands this. He joins the victims and this fascinating autobiography tells us that story, at least as far as he knows it. Mr. Frey is still a young man and we may assume that he will more fully understand the meaning of his dedication to Judaism as he grows in humanity. But the story of what he has done, the background of why he has done it, he shares with us here.

The context of Frey's attraction to Judaism is important for all of us, Jew and non-Jew alike. The Holocaust is surely the most important tragedy of our century. What does its mystery signify for us? Perhaps nothing that we can articulate. But Frey's response is one way of legitimately reacting to the Holocaust, just as this book is. We can be grateful that he is making this response.

PREFACE

We have chosen to compose what follows to accomplish several aims. One of those objectives was to coalesce and integrate our own thinking and feeling on the Holocaust. Another goal is to serve as a liaison between Academe and the general public on the subject of the extermination of the Jews of Europe. Foremost, however, was to present and discuss problems of moral, theological, academic, and personal importation deriving from the Holocaust that precious few scholars and theologians take time to ponder in print, much less act upon.

We expect critical review of our work herein; in fact, we would like nothing better than to have the conclusions to which the Holocaust has taken us shown to be in error. At least such demonstration would indicate that someone had read and thought about our ideas. We challenge novel thought and response to HaShoah. We have not reached the terminus of our search for an adequate response to the Holocaust; instead, that search remains quite open-ended. We feel that several items may be affirmed at this stage, however. Eradication of anti-Semitism (or, as these writers prefer, anti-Judaicism) will not prevent another Holocaust of the Jewish people. Buttressing existing institutions will not preclude the recurrence of mass death. Mankind had best not make freedom paramount for being human, for ultimately freedom in the context of operating in a world devoid of the Transcendent could cause the final solution to the human problem. Finally, the Holocaust is a <u>human</u> <u>problem</u> of overarching significance. The event must not be universalized away from its Jewish focus, yet response to it must encompass the entire human family.

The Occidental understanding of life encountered its most devastating dis-orienting experience in places such as Auschwitz, Babi Yar, and Treblinka. Reorientation of Western culture in response to the Holocaust must be away from the patterns of thought and institutional guidelines established and practiced over the past two hundred fifty years, the post-Enlightenment period of history. We have a sense of urgency about the work we have undertaken in this volume. Historical pseudo-revisionists press to construe the Holocaust as Jewish fantasy. Learned individuals ask what is special and different about the Holocaust, for indeed, have not men killed men before in countless numbers?

Why is not the destruction and terror of World War II sufficient cause to redirect mankind into more humane channels of behavior? Yet from the standpoint of morality, man has remained unchanged following both the Second World War and the Holocaust. In some small manner, perhaps we, through this work, can atone for the lack of response to the Holocaust.

ACKNOWLEDGMENTS

The authors wish to express their deepest appreciation to Daniel and Elaine Blank for the generous financial support which they lent to this effort. We also wish to thank Rabbi Irwin N. Goldenberg of Temple Beth Israel in York, Pennsylvania for his continual friendship and moral support.

Special note needs to be given Alice S. Diehl and Warren K.A. Thompson. Both of these individuals have long listened to our ideas and helped to sharpen our thinking. They are much more than friend and teacher.

We also want to extend our gratitude to the library staff of Lebanon Valley College for their perennial assistance in technical matters.

Finally, our thanks to Rory Paredes and Freelance Associates for their helpful suggestions and quality of work on our book.

INTRODUCTION

The approach used in this work, as will shortly be evident, combines two levels of expression: the personal and the scholarly. The reader will encounter use of the word _I_, a pronoun shunned in contemporary academic discourse. Choice of this approach was the result of conscious decision. Scholarly words about the Holocaust are of little value unless internalized in a specific person's mind. _I_ is an expression of the particular as opposed to the universal: it serves to personalize academic generalizations. What this book attempts to demonstrate is how one person's mind and soul and heart were touched by and responded to the Holocaust. That the statements contained in this work emanate from one mind should not render them valueless. _I_ gives the lessons of the Holocaust a human context and framework. The _I_ may help to reify the other detached, objective words used to discuss this <u>Awe-ful</u> Event.

CHAPTER I

THE RELEVANCE OF THE HOLOCAUST FOR HUMAN REFLECTION

The Holocaust(1) has become the most important platform of thought in my life. I have lived with this event cognitively, emotionally, and empathically for five years. Most days my mind is inexorably drawn to questions deriving from the Holocaust. I feel both weighed down and strangely lifted up when I ponder HaShoah.(2) I imagine that I feel uplifted psychologically because I know that Holocaust study is what should occupy a significant portion of my thinking. I have ceased to be a traveler in the Holocaust Kingdom, but am now a permanent denizen. The macabre scenes depicted in photographs and documentary footage now hold little of the fascination they once did. One learns that to be a serious student of the Holocaust, one must not ignore, but cannot focus upon, such scenes as the bulldozing of Jewish dead in the film Nuit et Brouillard.(3) However, from time to time, I feel compelled to look again at the photographic accounts of the Final Solution,(4) for pictures can sometimes convey what words cannot.(5) Particularly striking is one set of four photographs taken in close time proximity to each other.(6) They depict the annihilation of an entire Jewish community near the town of Kovel in the Soviet Union. Within minutes, the naked dead lie on the banks of the ravine. The machine guns are quiet, and there is silence. The people who were the essence of Jewish life in this small town lie bleeding on the earth. These photographs bring me back to a visceral level of response to the Holocaust. They remind me that aside from the historical theories explaining the rise of nazism and psychological reviews of the Hitlerite elite, the Holocaust was an event in the here and now, and of flesh and blood. | We who deal in words miss the point of the Holocaust if we abstract it out of the concrete realm of human event and suffering.| Concurrently, we do not lend assistance to understanding by dwelling on the unmitigated horror of the Holocaust. This is the problem with many photographs and much of the documentary footage available. Though human beings are presented therein, they are in bizarre positions of death or a terrifying condition of physical atrophy. To empathize better with this devastation, let us remind ourselves that a few short minutes or months prior to being photographed, the people were full-bodied, some intelligent and others slow, some comely and others plain. They were mothers and fathers, grandparents, and cherished little ones. They were people, each one a many-sided individual. Most contemporary Americans have little understanding of hunger, so we do not easily empathize with the emaciated figures shown in the liberation photographs of the various concentration camps(7) throughout Europe. The figures appear nonhuman, even ghoulish, and our hearts are not captured. What is called for in approaching and responding to the Holocaust is a healthy tension between the words and the people, abstractions and brutal reality. To think about the Holocaust is to consider it in abstract form; therefore, abstraction is inescapable. However, the abstraction is always in need of being rooted in an understanding of the human suffering and courage in the face of the Final Solution.

I have been sternly questioned as to the reason for my apparent fascination with the Holocaust, symbol of death in an incomprehensible amount. Why this fixation upon the morbid? I am asked. What would occupy my mental energy if this Holocaust business did not? others want to know. In response to the first query, I feel that I have gone far beyond the morbidity that initially attracts the sensationalist. Against the backdrop of the Holocaust, I am engaged in discerning what makes sense after such an event. I am in the process of determining what patterns of thought, mythic expession, and interpersonal behavior are to be nurtured in the light of HaShoah. I am using the Holocaust to ask questions about the nature of human beings and the direction of contemporary society. In this sense, I am indeed guilty of making the Holocust an abstraction, subject to mental manipulation. I do, however, try to reify the abstraction by periodic migration back to the particularity of Jewish suffering. I am patently not fixated upon the death that was the Holocaust, but rather am concerned with what will yield life after Auschwitz.(8) What can be affirmed about life given where and when the Holocaust occurred? What will serve to sustain life?

That a majority of my mental energies are channeled into Holocaust research and contemplation cannot be disclaimed. I cannot say what course those same energies would follow if I were not studying the Holocaust. More than likely I would be engaged in theological study, that is, being concerned with ultimate values. The Holocaust does fit my mental pattern of interest in human experiential extremes, be they ultimate values, agape,(9) cryogenics,(10) archeology, utopia, or the time-space continuum.(11) My primary purpose in writing about the Holocaust has been to learn precisely what I am thinking and feeling on this subject. Because I am forced to clarify my thoughts and feelings on HaShoah to the degree that they are discernible to other people, I learn about myself too. If I have discovered anything about the Holocaust, it is the enigmatic nature of this event. Just when thoughts coalesce into grander theories, another fragment of Holocaust knowledge shows the theory to be less than conclusive. An example of how my writing about the Holocaust precipitates the tightening of my thinking may serve well here. By thinking about the Holocaust, I had come to question the meaning of life. Because Auschwitz was a reality, how could life have any importance? It was through putting these general thoughts into words that I came to discover I was capable of affirming the value of life despite the Holocaust. I found I was also capable of affirming G-d despite Auschwitz. Neither affirmation, however, is without a sense of uneasiness and openness to emendation. I have seen myself grow and change with respect to Holocaust understanding within the context of my writing and study.

Yet I have been cautioned that Holocaust study is not a legitimate scholarly pursuit. I believe that the professor who made this statement to me was being genuinely pragmatic. He was concerned with the marketability of such specific academic expertise as a degree in Holocaust Studies. In the latter part of the 1970s, there was a graduate program in Holocaust Studies available through the Department of Religion at Temple University in Philadelphia.(12) It was this program of study to which the aforementioned professor issued his caveat to me. Yet I contend that there is much narrowness in the collective mentality of our society if it can find no place for one schooled in an interdisciplinary manner on the Holocaust. Obviously the powers-that-be in American Academe have not seen fit to recognize the legitimacy of a genuinely interdisciplinary approach to Holocaust study. Such study is evidently to be subsumed under the rubric of history, religion, or law -- which translates as adhering to established modes of inquiry. The study of the Holocaust does indeed involve rigorous academic standards. It cannot be taught or studied effectively in a shallow, anything-goes manner. However, the reality of the Holocaust is not encompassed by the academic discipline of history, though the event was an historical fact. Despite the G-d related problems raised by HaShoah, theological methodology cannot sufficiently explain or resolve the Holocaust. What is called for in the case of the Holocaust is academic study that flows easily through the rigid boundaries of academic disciplines. Each discipline has defined and guarded as its own a small segment of the universe of knowledge. Proponents within a given discipline do not take kindly to one extracting bits and pieces from their model of reality and then passing on to other disciplines to do the same. Yet Holocaust understanding beyond the superficial level can develop only when the well-defined academic walls are breached. I submit that Holocaust study in general, and the Holocaust event in particular, would be taken more seriously if several courageous universities would allow a space of legitimacy for Holocaust Studies as an interdisciplinary phenomenon. In this light, perhaps the graduate program at Temple University was indeed a courageous undertaking. Though not a thorough interdisciplinary course of study, the program nonetheless made the symbolic statement that the Holocaust is important enough to constitute a separate realm of study. The significance of the interdisciplinary approach cannot be overemphasized. Methods of inquiry and patterns of thought indigenous to philosophy, history, theology, law, science, and psychology all have value in learning about the Holocaust. The academic vehicles of response to HaShoah have primarily been historical and theological. There is pressing need, however, for response from philosophers and the scientific community as well.

I have been asked why I should so single-mindedly pursue Holocaust work. It is pointed out that I was not born Jewish. My family did not experience the power of the Hitler regime. I did not live through the period of 1933 to 1945. No one among my family, friends, or high school teachers ever talked about the systematic murder of the Jews of Europe. What possible connection could I have to the Holocaust to explain why my consciousness is infused with this event's abysmal solitude and utter paradoxes? Exposure to the Final Solution came initially from general curiosity about and interest in the Second World War. Briefly mentioned amidst the account of Allied victory and Nazi defeat were the war crimes trials(13) and the liberated concentration camps. Early recollections of mine include reading an article on Treblinka in Life magazine, along with the books Himmler and Ravensbrück.(14) In high school I can remember asking my parents to get Into That Darkness(15) for me, which they did. I do not believe they were aware of the content of that book, however. I did research on neo-nazism in contemporary Germany in senior high school. This was at a time when the Neo-Nazi party had captured significant numbers of delegate seats in the Bavarian state government. I am quite unsuccessful in reconstructing specific pathways towards my interest in the Holocaust. What I do know is that my ill-defined interest was coalesced during a course in college entitled "Ethics and the Holocaust".(16) The insight and direction which I derived from that seminar have served to guide my independent Holocaust study these past five years. Though I cannot untangle the sources of my interest, I do have profound commitment to Holocaust understanding. I firmly believe that from the Holocaust come questions of utmost significance for this generation and the next. The Holocaust survivors, Shlita,(17) may quickly respond that my commitment is all well and good, but I can turn my back on the reality of their suffering if I see fit. I can in my own mind make the Holocaust go away. My commitment, it can be claimed, lacks roots that give it living, though painful, meaning. Such possible charges against my dedication are indeed legitimate ones. What I feel I do possess, however, is the naivete to approach the Holocaust without the searing memories and be foolhardy enough to believe I can learn something from it. I have not been devoured from within by the terror of Auschwitz; I do not live the private non-hell(18) of the survivor. I am at best an observer, a recorder of images in the Holocaust Kingdom I never witnessed but have only heard about or read about in narrative and personal accounts. My very distance in historic time from the Holocaust may afford me the vantage point of visualizing the event as a totality rather than a fragment. For most of us who are not survivors, the Holocaust seems to have been a short-lived, violent disturbance upon the waters of history. Nothing but tiny ripples remain where once there had been waves of destruction. It is almost as if there had never been any waves. The survivor, standing on the shore, must wonder why all the other people around him on the sand do not fear those waters of history. And we, in turn, wonder wherein his anguish and apprehension lie. Why should we consider the Holocaust in particular, given the magnitude of death in the twentieth century alone?(19) Aren't there sufficient examples of man's inhumanity to man without isolating the Holocaust for special emphasis? There is certainly a good case to be made for placing the Holocaust within the continuum of human destructiveness.(20) Left without historical foundation, the Holocaust can be passed over as another example of peculiar events such as the sinking of the Atlantis. Conversely, without this benefit of context, the Holocaust can be considered so unique that nothing can be compared to it or drawn from it. The problem, however, with putting the Holocaust into the context of other human destructiveness is that it can be trivialized to the point of meaninglessness. The event loses its particularity of people and suffering in the morass of suffering-in-general.(21) The case for uniqueness(22) of the Holocaust event cannot be argued from the number of Jewish dead, for the Holocaust pales before the sheer quantitative weight of victims of twentieth century genocide. Certainly the fact that people died in the Holocaust, that is, death itself, does not delineate HaShoah from Hiroshima(23) or mass starvation in southern Asia. In all instances people died. If the number of dead in the Holocaust does anything, it renders us callous to death and suffering. If one hundred people are murdered, we may well be tempted to say that while their deaths were a tragedy, it is not as bad as six million dead. Playing this numbers game can lead one to very distorted conclusions about the Holocaust. In listening to a Jewish teacher talk to his seventh graders about HaShoah, I heard him make the point that the Gypsies lost nearly ninety-five percent of their population(24) whereas the Jews had lost a lesser percentage. The impression which I felt remained with his students was that the Jews came out ahead of the Gypsies in the Final Solution. Six million dead is as meaningless to people as one billion dollars. We can empathize with one person or several people dead, but we are as psychically numb(25) to six million dead as we are to the national debt figure of the United States. Yet following the modern trend to quantify everything, we still talk of the six million as if it will have any impact at levels of deeper perception. Death per se and the magnitude of death have thus been shown to be insufficient grounds to isolate the Holocaust for special emphasis. Why then is the Holocaust worthy of our undivided attention? The following points are platforms in establishing the relevance of the Holocaust for human reflection. The Final Solution was carried out by a legally instated government with the assistance of thousands of minor civil servants and bureaucrats. It was not the enterprise of a handful of madmen. The primary motivation behind the Nazi extermination program was not hatred or prejudice, but rather the rational completion of a stated defined goal. The Holocaust was conducted without the magnitude of hatred, depravity, and insanity so frequently imagined. The Jews were the prototype for state-defined superfluous and undesirable people;(26) not because of what they did or did not do politically, socially, or economically, but merely because they were Jewish. Jews were systematically hunted, registered, transported, and destroyed -- including men, women, and children. With a pre-war population of less than five percent of the total population of Germany, Jews posed no serious military, political, or social threat to the Nazi leadership. In addition to being few in number, German Jews by late 1930s had been stripped of their positions in government, education, and law. Despite the lack of threat emanating from the Jewish community in Germany, the Nazi elite proceeded with their program to remove the Jews from the face of Europe. A significant reason why there should be special emphasis placed upon the Holocaust over and above suffering-in-general is that it resulted from patterns of thought and institutions regarded to be among the best in the Western world.(27) In short, what allowed for the best accomplishments of the twentieth century also made possible the worst, namely Auschwitz. At Auschwitz, the Nazis engineered societies of total domination and dehumanization. Unlike people in the slave-holding colonies of pre-modern America, the prisoners had no value at all. What needs fine-grained examination are the intent, means, ideas, and forces that resulted in such ends as Dachau, Hiroshima, and continuing mass starvation in Asia. Qualitative difference among the three should emerge. I submit that the ultimate purpose for studying the Holocaust is to devise a kind of measuring stick for human behavior. If behavior or trend X can contribute to another Holocaust, its impact must be blunted or its direction altered. Because thought patterns and institutions regarded to be beneficial were involved in the Holocaust in some way, this event should constitute an imperative to radically reassess the direction of contemporary culture.

Several questions of moral import present themselves as appropriate to the discussion of the relevance of the Holocaust for human reflection. What is the difference between gassing Jews in Europe, and permitting significant numbers of people in poorer nations to starve to death each day. We do not hate the people who starve, but rather have normal indifference towards their well-being. As opposed to starvation, the gassing of Jews was a program with active participants.(28) The ethical line of demarcation

7

separating active murder and passive, distant observation of suffering is nebulous, but such delineation certainly is present in most codes of law. A witness who stands by and does nothing to aid, but also nothing to harm a victim, is not indicted for murder. The moral difference between the Nazi euthanasia program(29) and the Final Solution is even less concise than the case above. Late in the 1930s, six euthanasia installations were established wherein mentally and physically handicapped Germans, both childen and adults, were murdered. Though a step towards the Final Solution, the euthanasia program cannot be said to have involved the attempted eradication of a people and a way of life, in effect, the euthanasia effort was not genocide. It might be argued that in a world worried about global destruction from nuclear weapons, why should the Holocaust command our attention? By way of rebuttal to this contention, I submit that if there were to emerge from the Holocaust a radical redirection in thinking and behavior, the actual use of nuclear weapons would be more remote. The critical thinking that is called for in light of Auschwitz is not evident, however, when we prepare for war in the name of peace.(30) We delude ourselves into believing we are more secure with more expensive and dangerous weapons. When are we going to place value upon what those high-technology weapons are supposed to protect?

The Holocaust also requires special emphasis because it is being denied as an historical reality. What is it about this particular event that the pseudo-revisionist historians want to hide?(31) The thrust of the pseudo-revisionists is to call into question the legitimacy of Jewish suffering under the Nazis. Some of the claims issuing from the pseudo-revisionist camp include the following. There was no systematic extermination of the Jews by the Nazis; rather, such a contention is Zionist propaganda. "The typical inmate of a German concentration camp was a person being detained for punitive or security reasons."(32) "There is of course no direct documentary evidence for an extermination program."(33) This latter statement implies that no matter what a government perpetrates, if the planning and activities thereof are not documented in written form, the governmental action never occurred! I know of no other event of such historical magnitude that has been denied.(34) Most people, however, do not deny the historicity of the Holocaust. Yet what is offered by way of explanation for this event is usually quite simplistic. We as Americans are imbued with a spirit of social progress that does not easily mesh with mass killings and death factories. We take emotional refuge from the fact of six million Jewish dead by dismissing it as the work of a few madmen. We also accept the well-known apologetic of German economic ruin after the First World War as the cause for heightened anti-Semitism and the making of scapegoats of the Jews in Germany. Of the many people who were involved directly with the registration, deportation, and killing, we conclude they were simply following orders in the case of the military or not truly Christian in the civil servants. An emphasis is usually placed upon the sadism of camp guards and the bullying tactics of the Sturmabteilung.(35) The net result of these efforts is to explain the Holocaust in terms we can easily cope with and understand. If the Holocaust can be captured within the context of psychopathic behavior during a period of economic and political stress, we could all sigh with relief and return to the more pressing concerns of contemporary life. We would be very content to let things rest at the explanation of the Holocaust as another, albeit significant, instance of man's inhumanity to man. We might be prepared to grant that this event did involve the use of very technologically sophisticated means of killing; but nonetheless, it is explicable in terms with which we are familiar. For those of us who insist the Holocaust be treated separately from other human tragedies, we are reminded by the majority that the Nazi atrocities have been given the historically novel earmark of war crimes. Though the foregoing explanations do allow one glibly to place the Holocaust within the stream of twentieth century events, I submit that such accounts are historically shallow and indeed morally reprehensible. We certainly have many examples of man's inhumanity to his fellow man. An event of the magnitude of the Holocaust need not be used to ponder why bad things happen to good people. Such points are trite before the gates of Auschwitz. They can be drawn from any one of a hundred sources. To return momentarily to the economic and political stress apologetic for German action and moral inaction, it is precisely during times of stress that the fiber of institutions designed to deal with social tension is tested. Of what value are legal systems and organized religion, for example, if they do not function to maintain social homeostasis during periods of upheaval?

Allow me to clarify my position on the necessity for Holocaust reflection. What I see at Auschwitz is a synthesis of thought patterns and institutions with no moral direction.(36) When listed, these patterns of thought and institutions appear to be a summation of that which is regarded to be the best in our culture -- precisely because it is. I do not see the Holocaust resulting from anything going wrong with these thought patterns and institutions as we know them. Rather, it was because they went right that the Holocaust could occur! If the thought patterns, ideologies, and institutions of the Western world went right and still there was a Treblinka and a Sobibor, then the fundamental direction of Western civilization is in error. If this premise does not deserve our attention, little else will. When an assimilated group such as German Jewry is exterminated in civilized Europe in 1940 C.E.,(37) then we need to re-examine the shared values of humanity and the "safeguards" of civilization. This annihilation did not occur in the jungles of Paraguay(38) or Cambodia, but in the country of Bach and Beethoven.

Because the Holocaust was not revolutionary in the sense of sweeping ideational changes, political turnover, or economic collapse,(39) the thought patterns and institutions which led to its occurrence remain largely unchallenged and unchanged. For this reason, there remains the real possibility that a holocaust could occur again. We must exercise caution when making the previous statement if only to avoid a paranoid response to any socio-political changes. It should be apparent at this point that the Holocaust requires no Jewish special pleading to have intrinsic validity as a problem in need of much consideration. The Holocaust is a challenge of response for the entire Western world. The event is, foremost, a human dilemma. Ha-Shoah should not be appropriated by Jews alone, theologians alone, or historians alone. It was a public event that demands public attention. It occurred in the realm of physical reality; therefore, it cannot legitimately be removed from history and placed in an ethereal, theological domain. The Holocaust should also not become esoteric, the topic of discussion solely among scholars. Holocaust study enjoyed a popularity during the latter part of the 1970s that I do not believe it commands at this time. Despite the dangers of dilettantism that follows from popular appeal, confining the Holocaust to a few academic circles serves no one.

It is one thing to study the Holocaust in an academic manner; it is quite another matter to respond to the event in an holistic fashion. By holistic response is meant the combined involvement of one's mind, heart, and spirit in confronting the Holocaust. Just as the victims were people with many dimensions, so should our response to their deaths be on many different levels. In the course of my study and contemplation of the Holocaust, I have come to convert to Judaism from a firm background in Christianity. This pathway is not one I would suggest for anyone else, and certainly the Jewish rabbinical community would and did vehemently discourage such a decision. In addition to providing positive contributions to my life, my conversion to Judaism has inextricably linked me with the Holocaust. To be Jewish is to be touched at least peripherally by HaShoah. Though the Orthodox branch of Judaism plays down the significance of the Holocaust, the murder of one-third of the Jews alive in 1940 ultimately will have to find a place within the mainstream of Jewish memory and liturgy.

When asked what the Holocaust means to me personally, three things come to mind immediately. I think of fingernail marks, ashes, and a young girl. The fingernail marks refer to those indelibly clawed into the walls and ceilings of the gas chambers at Auschwitz. In a futile attempt to find air, people climbed on top of one another only to meet with the concrete ceiling. The Zyklon B crystals used at Auschwitz produced a gas that rose from the floor upwards. Fingernail marks in concrete record the last seconds of countless thousands of people. Ashes. Ashes by truckload were dumped into the Vistula River in Poland during the peak operation of Auschwitz in 1944. The ashes of parents and children, loved ones, strangers, rebbes and pupils. Ashes commingled into anonymity; the river washed away the memory. And finally, a young girl. Hanged at Auschwitz, her last words to the inmates as they filed past her were, "Remember me!" In a world filled with the results of our glorification of killing, this girl, in pathetic defiance, asked to be remembered. The watchword of the Jewish community after the Holocaust is "Remember", that the <u>Awe-ful</u> will never happen again. I contend that remembering is not enough with respect to the Holocaust. If our memories do not produce response and change within ourselves and the collective human community, then the memory of the Holocaust, in general, and of the young girl, in particular, is rendered meaningless. The Holocaust awaits our response.

11

NOTES

CHAPTER I

RELEVANCE OF THE HOLOCAUST
FOR HUMAN REFLECTION

1. The word Holocaust will be used in this volume to denote the dehumanization and annihilation of European and Soviet Jews during the period 1933-45. This destruction was carried out by thousands of people under the direction of the National Socialist (Nazi) elite of Germany. Though the Jews were the primary target of the Nazi killing program, many other peoples, groups, and individuals were murdered. Such groups included the Gypsies, Jehovah's Witnesses, Slavs, and Soviet and Polish intelligentsia and political elite.

2. HaShoah is an English transliteration of the Hebrew הַשׁוֹאָה, which means "the ruin, destruction, desolation, calamity". HaShoah will be used interchangeably with Holocaust in this work. For a detailed discussion of the terms which have been applied to the destruction of European Jews, see Alice Eckardt and A. Roy Eckardt, "Studying the Holocaust's Impact Today: Some Dilemmas of Language and Method," Judaism 27(1978): 222-32.

3. The film Nuit et Brouillard, directed by Alain Resnais, has French narration with English subtitles. Its English title is Night and Fog; the German title is Nacht und Nebel. Resnais combines scenes of the concentration camps as they appear today with documentary footage and photographs.

4. The Final Solution of the Jewish Question was the code name assigned by the German bureaucracy to the annihilation of the Jews of Europe.

5. One of the most striking collections of photographs relating to the Holocaust is found in Harry James Cargas, A Christian Response to the Holocaust.

6. Martin Gilbert, The Holocaust, pp. 39-40.

7. The general conception of the concentration camps is that these were a monolithic phenomenon, that is, that they were all basically similar. This notion is inaccurate. There were specifically Death Camps, all of which were located in Poland. The Death Camps

12

were Treblinka, Sobibor, Auschwitz-Birkenau, Chelmno, Belzec, and Maidanek. These camps were established for the sole purpose of murdering Jews and other peoples. In addition to the Death Camps, there were spread throughout Europe concentration camps, often with satellite slave labor camps associated with them. Examples of such concentration camps were Mauthausen (Austria), Buchenwald (Germany), and Natzweiler (France). The first Nazi concentration camp was established in 1933 at Dachau in southern Germany. The original inmates there were political prisoners. Though there was much death and suffering within the concentration camps, only the six Death Camps were designed specifically as killing centers for large numbers of people. Concentration camps in general may be considered to have been societies in which the object was total domination and dehumanization of the people therein. It is noteworthy that all of the killing centers and many of the concentration and slave labor camps were not located within Germany itself.

8. Auschwitz will be used as an alternative word for Holocaust in this book. Being the largest and most complex of the concentration camps, Auschwitz has come to symbolize the Holocaust in much historical and theological literature.

9. Agape refers to the ultimate form of love of which G-d alone is capable -- extending love with no expectation of return. Agape is selfless love at its finest.

10. Cryogenics involves study and observations of phenomena that occur in extreme cold. An example of the practical application of cryogenics is the deep-freezing of terminally ill people until the time at which their illnesses are curable.

11. The time-space continuum relates to my interest in ultimates and extremes in that it involves such questions as, What happens to time at speeds approaching that of light? and How do speeds approaching that of light affect our perception of objects, sound, and mass. For the physicist, the speed of light is the ultimate speed that energy can attain.

12. The Holocaust Studies program at Temple University was founded and nurtured by Dr. Franklin H. Littell. The program was a course of study leading to a Ph.D. Holocaust Studies was but one possible area of concentration of the four required to complete a degree

in religion. The Holocaust program had its first graduate in 1982, but it has subsequently dissolved due to faculty disinterest.

13. War crimes trials refer to public trials of major Nazi war criminals held from 20 November 1945 until 1 October 1946. Delegates from the United States, France, the Soviet Union, and Great Britain served as members of the International Military Tribunal. The trials were held before the tribunal in Nuremberg, Germany. The purpose of the Nuremberg Court was to provide a legal, ordered environment in which to examine the evidence against the Nazi elite. For further discussion of the Nuremberg war crimes trials, see Bradley F. Smith, Reaching Judgment at Nuremberg. An article on the notion of war crimes is that of C.C. Aronsfeld, "The Extermination of the Jews Was No 'War Crime'," Contemporary Review 231 (1977): 145-48. Aronsfeld contends that the Nazi program against the Jews had nothing to do with war except that it was carried out during one. He argues that the Final Solution was a distinct effort merely effected under the cloak of wartime disorder. Other Holocaust scholars point to the fact that the killing of Jews actually hindered the German war effort by draining off essential transportation and bureaucratic resources. Trains were diverted from strictly military usage to transport Jews to Auschwitz and the German bureaucratic system was burdened with the logistics of such an enterprise.

14. Germaine Tillion, Ravensbrück.

15. Gritta Sereny, Into That Darkness.

16. The course, "Ethics and the Holocaust", was offered by the philosophy department at Lebanon Valley College in Annville, Pennsylvania. The instructor for that seminar, Mr. Warren K. Thompson, has been a source of continual support and encouragement for my research and writing on the Holocaust.

17. Shlita is an acronym formed from the Hebrew Sheyichye leyomum tovim aruchim, "May he live a good and long life".

18. I chose to use non-hell instead of simply hell because hell is used to denote the final spiritual state of the ungodly. See Matt. 10: 28 and Mark 9: 43 for such usage in the Christian canon. Hell implies punishment for wrongdoing and unrighteousness. The Jews of Europe were not killed because they had done

anything wrong. On the contrary, they were killed because they had affirmed their Jewishness and/or their grandparents had done so. The Nazis defined a Jew to be anyone with practicing Jewish grandparents as far back as 1870. To speak of a survivor's personal hell; therefore, is to suggest that his suffering was deserved.

19. For insight into the magnitude of genocide in the twentieth century, see Gil Eliot, Twentieth Century Book of the Dead.

20. An illustration of placing the Holocaust within the continuum of human destructiveness is Richard L. Rubenstein, The Age of Triage.

21. See Emil L. Fackenheim, "Jewish Faith and the Holocaust: A Fragment," Commentary 46(1968): 30-36 for a discussion of the Holocaust and the suffering-in-general motif.

22. For a treatment of the uniqueness of the Holocaust in theological terms, see A. Roy Eckardt, "Is the Holocaust Unique?," Worldview 17(1974): 31-35.

23. The Japanese city of Hiroshima was the first city to be destroyed in war by an atomic bomb. The bomb was dropped from an aircraft there on 6 August 1945.

24. It is noteworthy that in past centuries, Gypsies have been associated with Jews in both popular European belief and in scholarly investigation. The Nazis engaged two bureaucratic agencies in researching the racial connection of Gypsies and Jews. For a view of the Gypsies in contemporary Germany, see "The Nazis' Forgotten Victims," Time, 19 November 1979, p. 58.

25. An expression borrowed from Dr. Robert J. Lifton.

26. The concept of state-defined superfluous populations is developed in Richard L. Rubenstein, The Cunning of History, pp. 14-16.

27. Several scholars write from the premise that the Holocaust was essentially a rational event that must be understood as part of mainstream Western civilization. See John T. Pawlikowski, "The Holocaust As Rational Event." Reconstructionist 40(1974): 7-14; George M. Kren and Leon Rappoport, The Holocaust and

the Crisis of Human Behavior; and Rubenstein, Cunning of History.

28. The gassing of Jews refers to the method of killing that involved cyanide gas or carbon monoxide gas. The method of gas-killing evolved first from mobile carbon monoxide vans, then to carbon monoxide chambers, and finally to cyanide gas chambers. The crystals which produced the cyanide gas were marketed as Zyklon B and generally were sold to exterminate vermin and insects in closed areas. The Zyklon was produced by two private companies, the Dessauer Werke and the Kaliwerke. Werke translates from the German as "industrial works". For additional information, see Raul Hilberg, The Destruction of the European Jews.

29. The euthanasia centers were located at Bernberg, Brandenburg, Grafeneck, Hadamar, Hartheim, and Sonnestein. All of these installations were within the borders of Germany. It is noteworthy that the euthanasia program was disbanded in the wake of vocal protest emanating from the clergy and general public in Germany and abroad. This runs counter to the idea that world outcry on behalf of the Jews would not have effected any policy changes by the Nazi elite. See Lucy S. Dawidowicz, The War Against the Jews 1933-1945, pp. 175-80.

30. This thought was borrowed from Herbert Marcuse, One Dimensional Man.

31. There is a well funded system in America and Europe which seeks to establish by scholarly means that the Holocaust did not happen in any way conformable to histories of that event written by Raul Hilberg, Lucy S. Dawidowicz, and Gerald Reitlinger. Under the guise of academic legitimacy, the Institute for Historical Review in Torrance, California has published many books and pamphlets denying the reality of Jewish death and suffering under National Socialism that resulted from a program of extermination. It should be noted that legitimate historical revisionism does exist. There has been much written from the revisionist viewpoint regarding the American Civil War, for example, that challenges the consensus accounts of the war. Revisionists tend to see one of the primary causes of the Civil War being the North's economic domination of the South. A main platform in the consensus approach is that the war was fought to abolish slavery.

32. Arthur R. Butz, The Hoax of the Twentieth Century, p. 36.

33. Ibid., p. 19.

34. Two other examples of the virulently anti-Jewish and anti-historical accounts of the Holocaust which are circulating in America and Europe are Paul Rassinier, Debunking the Genocide Myth; and Wilhelm Staeglich, The Auschwitz Myth. For additional information on the pseudo-revisionist camp, see Lucy S. Dawidowicz, "Lies About the Holocaust," Commentary 70(1980): 31-37; "Author To Be Stripped of Doctorate," Baltimore Jewish Times, 15 April 1983, p. 31; and Franklin H. Littell, "A Report on Historical 'Revisionism'," mimeographed (Philadelphia: National Institute on the Holocaust, 1981). Dr. Littell's address was first presented at the International Council of Yad Vashem in Jerusalem. Yad Vashem is a combination memorial, museum, archive, and research center dedicated to the memory of the six million Jewish dead of the Holocaust.

35. Sturmabteilung (SA) were referred to as Brown Shirts or Storm Troopers. They were the private army of the National Socialist party (Nationalsozialistische Deutsche Arbeiterpartei or NSDAP), and were well known for their terrorist and bullying activities. The SA were largely responsible for Kristallnacht, the "Night of Broken Glass", which occurred 9-10 November 1938. It was on Kristallnacht that the storefronts of Jewish-owned businesses throughout Germany were smashed, synagogues set afire, and Jewish men arrested and interned in Buchenwald, Dachau, and Sachsenhausen concentration camps. Nearly one hundred Jews died in this pogram, with many more being injured. An unknown number of Jewish women were raped. Of note is the fact that of those Nazi party members brought before civilian courts for their crimes during Kristallnacht, only those convicted of raping a Jewish woman were imprisoned and stripped of party membership. In the Nazi ideology, sexual intimacy with Jews was the worst crime an Aryan could commit.

36. The thought patterns and institutions to which I alluded are the concept of universal man, science, bureaucracy, capitalism, organization, rationality, human intelligence, technology, modern language, education, law, professionalism, humanism, and the Enlightenment idea of progress. Further explanation of each is contained in subsequent chapters.

37. C.E. refers to the common era or Christian era dating from the birth of Jesus of Nazareth.

38. For an account of the murder of innocent members of the Ache Indian tribes of Paraguay, see Richard Arens, ed., Genocide in Paraguay. The primary motivation for killing the native population seems to be for their land. On a note related to Paraguay, the infamous Dr. Josef Mengele who had been at Auschwitz is living in Paraguay and reportedly has resumed his medical experimentation on the Indians there. See Richard Arens, "Dr. Mengele's New Victims," New York Times, 28 March 1979, p. A24.

39. That the Holocaust was not a visible revolution is a theme developed in Kren and Rappoport, Holocaust and Crisis of Behavior. The final chapter of their volume, "The Holocaust and the Human Condition", is of particular significance.

CHAPTER II

THE HOLOCAUST
AS IT MIGHT AFFECT CHRISTIAN THEOLOGY

The annihilation of European and Soviet Jews from 1933 to 1945 is an event which all denominations of the contemporary Christian Church(1) must recognize as significant. Why this has to be so is not at all obvious to many people who profess the Christian faith and, therefore, must be demonstated prior to a discussion of how the event was significant. I do not wish to convey the idea that there has been no sensitive Christian response to the Holocaust. There have been notable beginnings made by such Christian scholars(2) as Franklin H. Littell,(3) A. Roy Eckardt,(4) John T. Pawlikowski,(5) Rosemary Ruether,(6) and Harry James Cargas.(7) There have also been official Church statements as to the kinship of Judaism and Christianity and on the moral wrong of anti-Semitism.(8) However, the impact of the Holocaust as an event posing problems for Christian theology and Christian people has not begun to reach the laity level,(9) and is also much lacking among the pastorate.

One is confronted with developing reasons for isolating the Endlösung(10) as one of the most disorienting(11) experiences for the Christian Church in twenty centuries. What is it about the Holocaust that should cause Christians to extract it from all of the other human suffering which has occurred over the years, and invest this event with intrinsic meaning? Why should Jewish suffering initiate Christian theological and moral issues? There are several salient reasons for specifically a Christian response to a problem which appears to be a Jewish one. First, there was a direct involvement of practicing Christians in the National Socialist (Nazi) extermination program. One of the commanders of the mobile killing units which destroyed entire Jewish communities in the western Soviet Union was a pastor.(12) Unlike the common notion that the Holocaust was carried out by fanatics and madmen, the thousands of civil servants and bureaucrats who made the extermination process work on a daily basis were often ordinary Christians. To consider the Holocaust as an event requiring special Christian emphasis solely because of Christianity's direct complicity therein presents difficulty in the light of Christian involvement in the enslavement of blacks and in the destruction of American Indian cultures.(13)

19

These events, however, stand in sharp relief against the enduring and complex tradition of Christian theological anti-Judaicism. Twenty centuries of anti-Judaic Christian teaching and practice provided a very fertile medium upon which the Nazis relied to carry out the Final Solution.(14) The deep-seated attitudes which developed from such anti-Judaic teachings contributed to Christian complicity in, and Christian silence to, the murder of millions of Jewish men, women, and children. We should recognize that Adolf Hitler did not engineer the Endlösung in an atheistic desert, but rather in the heart of Christendom. I do not believe that there exists a direct pathway from the Christian Gospels to Auschwitz.(15) However, I do believe that it can be strongly argued that Christianity provided an extensive fund of negative images of the Jew.(16) Such negative images helped to create Christian moral indifference to Jewish suffering in the 1930s and 1940s. The power of these images of the Jew derives in part because they were given religious sanction.(17) In addition, they derive power from the pervasive ignorance of Judaism on the part of Christian clergy and laity. Most Christians are unaware of Jewish life and religious practice other than from the Gospel accounts. Because Christians have little knowledge of living Judaism, they cannot effectively counter theologically and scripturally-supported anti-Judaic images. For many Christians, Judaism was surpassed as a religious reality in the first century of the common era(18) by the emerging Church. Jewish struggles, ideas, and metamorphosis throughout the ensuing centuries often remain untaught in Sunday schools and adult religious education classes. Yet the most profound basis upon which the Christian Church might begin its response to the Holocaust is the knowledge that Christianity is linked to the heritage of no other people as it is to that of the Jews. Christianity cannot establish an identity that does not include a rich historical and *living* relationship with the Jewish people. Therefore, Christian involvement in and silence to the mass murder of Jews, the very people from whom is derived theological perspective and spiritual sustenance, strikes at a basic level -- as son to father. It should also be remembered that Jesus of Nazareth was an observant Jew all his life. These reasons serve to demonstrate why the Holocaust of the Jews should receive special Christian emphasis. There are, however, several major barriers which stand in the way of Christian consideration of the Holocaust as a monumental event. The first of these obstacles is the traditional

Christian concept of history.(19) The Christian historical model is one in which the Resurrection of Jesus and his Second Advent are two towering peaks. Stretched out from the base of these peaks is all the rest of human history. When placed within this historical scheme, the Holocaust is part of the plateau of human experience, but does not in any way alter the two major events by which all history is measured. Several questions emerge for consideration at this point. Is faith the guideline by which history is measured? or, conversely, Is human history, of which the Holocaust is part, the guideline by which faith is measured?(20) Should events in the here and now affect our faith? Is it defensible to change what we can affirm about G-d as a result of what has happened in earthly history? Is Christian theology subject to tellurian experience? Certainly there is ample biblical justification for subjecting faith to the judgment of history. Jews and Christians alike have affirmed that G-d acts through the happenings of particular time and place. Therefore, what happens in earthly history has indeed been viewed to be significant. The Exodus of the Jewish people from Egypt is an example of historic event interpreted as a direct action of G-d in the context of history. Christianity is also prepared to accept direction from a <u>concrete</u> <u>event</u> in the first century, namely, the Crucifixion.

Just as the traditional Christian model of history makes response to the Holocaust more difficult, so do the traditional Christian interpretations of evil. The Christian theologian John H. Hick, when writing specifically about the Jewish martyrs of the Holocaust, found justification for this evil in the amount of good to which it will lead at the end of time.(21) Though Hick does not see the extermination of six million Jews as G-d's will, he does believe the victims "will have their place in the final fulfillment of God's creation."(22) The Holocaust is thus reduced to another one of the multitude of human tragedies that will be transposed into goodness and glory at the terminus of time.

For the Christian Church to apply the age-old deuteronomic formula,(23) that evil is punished and good is rewarded, to the Holocaust event is both inappropriate and insensitive. Seen in the deuteronomic motif, Jewish suffering under the Nazis would be a result of wrongdoing on the part of the victims. Graphic example of such insensitivity is provided in

21

the declaration issued by the council of the Evangelical Church of Germany regarding the Jews at the council's Darmstadt Conference in April, 1948.(24) The declaration asserted that the suffering of the Jews under the Nazi rule was G-d's punishment for Jewish rejection of Christ. The deuteronomic formula interprets suffering in terms of cause and effect, guilt and retribution. Such traditional insight will not afford Christianity the vision to integrate the Holocaust into its collective mentality.

Christianity has been extremely reluctant to recognize any divine revelation following the life, death, and Resurrection of Jesus of Nazareth. This unwillingness to accept theologically an on-going divine-human encounter(25) is another obstacle to Christians deriving meaning from the Holocaust. The theologian Jürgen Moltmann is seen by some scholars as being a proponent of the traditional stance on revelation. For Moltmann, "the event of Golgotha(26) remains the solely decisive event of salvation-history. Yet how is it possible for us to remain bound by that single event? How can we stop at that place? Are we not called to find in the subsequent unfolding of events an acting out of the divine-human encounter, and hence of the human understanding of God?"(27) It was Christian interpretation of events which maintained that revelation did not cease at Sinai;(28) therefore, contemporary Christians cannot logically conclude that all revelation stopped with Jesus. According to the theme set forth in Robert McAfee Brown's book, The Pseudonyms of God,(29) Deity reveals itself in a multitude of different ways. It would appear to be an anthropomorphic limiting of G-d if we humans were to maintain that revelation reached its ultimate zenith in Jesus. Let us instead hope for the continued outpouring of G-d's revelation and support for mankind. Christianity needs to recognize precisely what it claims to affirm; namely, that G-d acts in the confines of particular time and place. By doing this, Christianity would then be open to theological learning and re-definition from specific historic events. It must be remembered that G-d does not only act through good people and churchmen, but He also communicates through such insignificant entities as a burning bush.(30)

Let us consider a fourth impediment to Christianity coming to grips with the Holocaust as an event significant specifically for Christian people. The individual Christian holds the idea that no one, in practice, can fulfill all of the Christian precepts.

He will argue that there is no such person as a true Christian because all people fall short of emulating Christ in their daily lives. Just as the individual Christian will claim that everyone falls short of the ideal in practice, the Christian theologian will contend that the original and true Christian kerygma(31) was misinterpreted throughout the centuries. Subsequent practice based upon a departure from the true Christian message is thus seen not to be a reflection of the original proclamation of Good News. Yet Harry James Cargas reminds us that "people are the church";(32) therefore, the practice of theology, the human expression thereof, is the one element to be considered. It is not sociologically justifiable to maintain that one's religion is inherently valid, but its practice has gone wrong. "The 'crucified Christ' simply cannot be separated from what has happened to, and been done to, the Cross."(33) We shall now consider some instances of Christian theologians using the misinterpretation apologetic to explain Christian involvement in HaShoah. The Roman Catholic theologian Hans Küng, while acknowledging the fact of Nazi persecution of the Jews, claims that the concentration camp guards and those people directly involved in murder were "not truly Christian". He makes this claim despite the fact that those same Germans, Austrians, and Poles regarded themselves as Christians.(34) What difference does it make if Christianity in some pristine form is good, but its human application is harmful to Jews and others?, and by what guideline is "true Christian practice" measured? Harry James Cargas raises similar questions when he asks whether one can "be a Christian today, given the death camps which, in major part, were conceived, built and operated by a people who called themselves Christians...It is too easy to say of those who lived and persecuted or remained 'neutral' in Germany... and other nations during the Nazi era that, although they regarded themselves as Christians, they really weren't. That's too smug an answer."(35)

The church historian and theologian Franklin H. Littell in his volume, The Crucifixion of the Jews, asserts that "the Holocaust was the consummation of centuries of false teachings and practice..."(36) (The underlining is my own.) False teachings and practice, of course, refer to the teachings and practice based upon the "New Testament". Dr. Littell evidently interprets the devolution of some of the Church's teaching into theological anti-Semitism as being a result of a misapplication or misinterpretation of the true Christian message. Much effort is expended in determining whether the Gospels are inherently anti-Semitic, or if the churches after 70 C.E. assumed an anti-Judaic stance for ecclesiastical and political reasons. In their critical review essay of Rosemary Ruether's Faith and Fratricide, Thomas A. Idinopulos and Roy Bowen Ward concur with Dr. Ruether that the basis of anti-Judaic thought was laid in the "New Testament".(37) However, they point out that "hostility towards Jews and Jewish religion in the Greco-Roman world antedated Christianity"(38), thereby implying that the Church writers merely adopted an older prejudice and adapted it to their own purposes. What needs to be recognized is that the system of Christianity cannot be evaluated independently of its human manifestations. It can be argued that, for whatever reasons, the record of Christianity has been decidedly, and not infrequently, violently anti-Judaic. No appeal to "intrinsic good" can erase twenty centuries of historic event. Christianity must accept responsibility for its members' actions.

The final obstacle to Christian response to the Holocaust with which we will deal in this work is the traditional Christian focus upon the next world, the world to come. I do not wish to imply that all Christian people or all Christian denominations have no concern for events in the here and now. What is meant is that, throughout its history, the Christian Church has tended to emphasize the vertical component of life -- the relationship of man to G-d in heaven.(39) In need of development is the horizontal component, that is, man's relationship to the rest of the human community. The material realm (things of the earth) has been held in low esteem by the Church in contradistinction to the spiritual domain. Too long has the Augustinian principle of viewing the world as sub ratione peccati, "under sin",(40) held influence in the collective Christian mind. This world has traditionally been equated with sin, the flesh, baseness, carnal desire, temporalness, evil, material cares, and secularism. The Roman Catholic theologian Friedrich Heer in his volume, God's First Love, perceives these negative images of this world to be the sources of fatalism in the Christian tradition.

The withdrawal of the Church from history has created that specifically Christian and ecclesiastical irresponsibility -- towards the world, the Jew, the other person, even the Christian himself, considered as a human being, -- which was the ultimate cause of past catastrophes and may be the cause of the final catastrophe in the future.(41)

Christianity must understand that the same world it too often downgrades is the one in which we all must live and attempt to make intelligible. If this world is dismissed as having little importance, where does this leave us? This world, though it be temporal in terms of man's existence, cannot continue to be seen only as a way station to heaven. The churches should not, in the words of Franklin H. Littell, continue their "flight from history". How can the Holocaust or any event occurring at a particular point in time and space have any meaning in a framework in which only the spiritual dimension has importance value?

On a related theme, Christianity has been imbued with the spirit of apocalypticism since its beginnings. The apocalyptic viewpoint is but one way of looking at the direction of temporal history. According to this viewpoint, G-d will intervene directly in the affairs of men when conditions on earth get too bad for people to solve on their own. The apocalyptic perspective tends to make people rely on G-d for help in all situations. It may be argued that the Holocaust constitutes definite proof that man is unable to change the world for the better, and therefore, must rely solely upon G-d and not himself. A more fitting contention, however, is that this event provided substantial evidence that G-d will not intervene in the affairs and history of man in Deus ex machina(42) fashion despite the level of man's descent into evil. In addition, the Holocaust event demonstrates that G-d will not take the side of the innocent against the forces of darkness. Miracle(43) becomes an untenable postulate in light of Auschwitz. These points are not presented to argue that man has no need of Deity,(44) or that he himself possesses unlimited potential. However, faith in G-d's control of human history divorced from responsibility for one's actions is not a valid stance after the Holocaust. Also, faith cannot be seen as a legitimate reason for social inaction. The contemporary Christian must perceive himself to be an active agent within the human community and not merely the passive recipient of a salvation formula. In effect, the post-Holocaust Christian can no longer claim to "be saved", and then expect G-d to take care of everything else. One must not permit himself the luxury of what the theologian Dietrich Bonhoeffer(45) termed "cheap grace". Just as individual Christians must see their actions as meaningful and important in a social sense, so the contemporary Christian Church must direct its efforts back into the continuum of earthly time and event. A passage from the Hebrew prophet Micah (Mic. 6:8) combines both man's need for G-d and his responsibility to other men. "And what does the Lord require of you but to do justice, and to love kindness, and to walk privately(46) with your God?"

Hopefully having demonstrated the urgent need for Christian response to the Holocaust along with the problems inherent in that search, we will now suggest possible pathways that response process might follow. A starting point on the road to sensitive Christian response would be for the Church to recognize HaShoah as a new revelation.(47) The Holocaust needs to become a source of growth, change, and social commitment for the Christian community. Revelation might begin as a different Christian understanding of the Jewish people and of Judaism. The Holocaust of the Jews should reveal to the Christian that his faith derives sustenance and historical identity from Judaism. Judaism is not merely a theological anchor for the Christian tradition!(48) Instead, the Jewish faith must be seen as a complete religious reality, able to stand on its own merit. The Church must not only recognize its Jewish heritage, but it must learn of that heritage and teach it from sources other than the Apostolic Writings and the Letters of Paul.(49) The Christian "New Testament" is not the resource from which Christians can gain an accurate and detailed, much less positive, account of first century Judaism. Certainly contemporary Jewish practice is not to be discerned from the "New Testament" either. It is impossible to mentally construct an accurate concept of living Jews from the Gospel accounts. For Christians to gain an understanding of Jews and Judaism today, human intercontact is essential. Church groups and Sunday school classes might regularly visit Jewish houses of worship(50) to become familiar with modern Jewish religious expression. Insofar as Christians learning about first century Judaism, specifically Jewish sources on that time period need to be consulted. Following the Holocaust, Jews may be understandably reluctant to open the doorway to communication with the Christian community. Some Jewish writers simply have asked Christians to let Jews alone, period.(51) It will require perseverance on the part of concerned Christians to break down the barrier of mistrust which has been built over the centuries. I

26

believe the major burden of bridge-building between the Jewish and Christian communities lies with the Christian Church and Christian people.

The Holocaust should also reveal to Christians that Jews have maintained their steadfastness to G-d's covenant. The Christian Church needs to affirm Jewish <u>steadfastness</u> to G-d as opposed to the all too prevalent theme of Jewish <u>rejection</u> of Christ. Christian Holocaust scholars have argued convincingly that the triumphalist claim advanced by the early Church and kept alive throughout history provided the structure upon which theological anti-Semitism grew. The essence of the triumphalist claim is that G-d is finished with the Jews as a people because they failed to recognize Jesus of Nazareth as the awaited Messiah.(52) The Church, therefore, has replaced the Jewish people as the bearers of G-d's covenant.(53) By making the triumphalist claim, the Church views itself as the chosen vehicle of G-d's work in the world. It must be remembered, however, that the Jews died in the Nazi Final Solution because they had been faithful to the same covenant which Christianity claims to have appropriated as its own. The Nazi racial theorists had defined a Jew to be anyone with practicing Jewish grandparents as far back as 1870. Imagine a Jewish person born in 1850, who, twenty years later in 1870, makes the conscious decision to detach himself from his family's religion and way of life to become Christian. His grandchildren and great grandchildren would not be gassed seventy years later because they were Jews. This, of course, is not to say that they would not have been interned or killed for political or health reasons.(54) Now let us consider a similar Jewish individual, born in 1850. He instead maintains his observance of Judaism, his belief in G-d, his study of the Torah. Precisely because he had been steadfast to the Jewish people's thirty-five hundred year-old covenant with G-d, his grandchildren may well perish at Auschwitz. They would die because their grandfather had been steadfast in his relationship with G-d.

Not only does Christian triumphalism allow no theological space for Judaism today, but this false claim blinds Christians to the reality of living Jews and Jewish practice. Many Sunday school curricula support the notion that contemporary Jews are beings left-over from another age. Support comes in the form of little or no mention of the growth and change within the Jewish tradition since the Destruction of the Temple in 70 C.E. by the Romans.(55) So that Jews and

Judaism today are not perceived to be anachronisms, Church school lessons need to present accurate information about such topics as the growth of rabbinic Judaism since Pharisaic times, the development of the Talmud, and the emergence of Jewish mysticism. Such teaching about Judaism would best be presented by a rabbi. Eva Marie Fleischner, a Christian professor of religion at Montclair State College in New Jersey, has offered this commentary on triumphalism. "I do not see how, in the face of the Holocaust, we can continue in our arrogant Christian claim of superiority. What is called for are compunction of heart and confession of our sinfulness, in the knowledge that God's love and mercy are infinitely greater yet, and can indeed transform our hearts of stone into hearts of flesh (Ezekiel 36)."(56)

The Holocaust should make apparent the urgent need for genuine communication between Christians and Jews. Any discussion of Jewish-Christian relationship necessarily involves the Christian Gospels -- the books of Matthew, Mark, Luke, and John. Yet how is the Church to deal with certain anti-Judaic passages in the Gospel accounts following HaShoah? Some Christian theologians have suggested the removal of anti-Jewish verses from the Christian canon. This seems to be too radical an approach to hope to meet with any measurable success; for, in the final analysis, it amounts to censorship. If the call is issued to censor the "New Testament", then that same appeal might be applied to Shakespeare's literature (57) and Goethe's Faust as well. Plays, prose, sculpture, poetry, and all art forms would cease to be expressions of an artist's heart and mind, but instead reflect a censor's uniform contour. How much more should sacred literature be exempt from censorship, even in the name of combatting anti-Semitism! The challenge remains, however, of how to end or reduce the animosity of Christian towards Jew which is supported by the Gospels. A beginning step would be for Christian theologians and clergy to emphasize those Gospel passages which speak of the Jewish people in a positive light.(58) In addition, could not both oral and written commentary be developed within the Christian tradition that would serve to update, explain, and temper the Scriptures? Commentary on sacred writings is not a novelty. Within Judaism, there are commentators such as Rashi,(59) the Rambam,(60) and the Ramban(61) who have reinterpreted and updated the Torah. In the Jewish tradition, commentary is invested with almost as much authority as the scripture itself. If

Christianity did develop commentary on its canon, pastors and priests could then use this to offset the anti-Judaic passages of the Gospels in the context of the liturgy.(62) Clergy would have a tool to sensitize members of their congregations to the negative implications of certain Gospel verses. The impact of this commentary would be heightened if it is given sanction and acceptance in the worship service. The practical effects of Christian commentary on the Gospels would be a reduction in the fund of negative images of the Jew, and consequently, a decline in Christian moral indifference towards the Jewish people.

It must be reiterated that the credibility of the Gospel record vis-a-vis first century Jewish thought, activity, and ritual is extremely tenuous. I am categorically not saying, or implying, that the Gospels impart no truth. However, the treatment of Jews and Judaism therein is quite suspect in terms of historical accuracy. A volume by Haim Cohn(63) titled The Trial and Death of Jesus is apropos to this issue. Cohn's work contains discussion of the three years of Jesus' ministry, with particular focus upon His trial and death. Haim Cohn's treatment of this topic utilizes legal methodology based on neutral and reliable sources about the Jewish and Roman laws and customs of the first century period. One example of Cohn's legal analysis of the Gospels involves Matthew 27:24-25 in which the Roman governor Pontius Pilate washes his hands of responsibility for Jesus' execution, claiming Jesus to be innocent. The Jewish crowd, standing before Pilate's residence, then is said to have shouted: "His blood be on us and our children." Cohn argues that Pilate's washing his hands of guilt and complicity in a death he supposedly feels to be unjust is a Hebrew and not a Roman practice. Pilate would not have declared his innocence in front of a crowd of natives, as he was the viceroy of the Caesar himself. It would have been beneath Pilate's dignity to explain himself to a group of townspeople in a Roman province. Cohn asserts that the cry from the Jewish crowd, "His blood be on us and our children," would have made no impression upon Pilate. It was Pilate's decision alone to execute or free Jesus. It is noteworthy that none of the other Gospel writers besides "Matthew" include the cry of the crowd in their accounts of the Crucifixion. This cry has been used by the Church throughout its history to explain Jewish suffering. The recurrent theme within Christian tradition of Jewish rejection of Jesus is undercut when it is remembered that the majority of Jews alive at the time of Jesus did not live in

Palestine. There were major Jewish communities in Egypt, Greece, and Asia Minor. Most of the Jews of the first century would never have known about Jesus to accept or reject him!

Another point that Haim Cohn discusses in his work is the Gospel writer's placement of Jesus in tension with the Pharisees of His day. The Pharisees are portrayed as not accepting Jesus' contention that sick people should be helped and healed on the Sabbath.(64) Acording to Cohn, this portrayal is inaccurate because there exists a rabbinic injunction specifically obligating one to help the sick or dying on the Sabbath. The Gospel account is superficially credible on this point because of the commandment in the Jewish tradition forbidding "work" on the Sabbath. The Pharisees are presented as objecting to Jesus' argument to help the sick on the grounds that healing is "work". Tension between Jesus and one group of the religious authorities of the day was an important theme for the Gospel writers to develop. If, as the Church claims, Jesus' message on earth was new and fundamentally distinct, then the early writers had to show Jesus in opposition with the Jewish religious elite. Following the ashes of Auschwitz and Treblinka, it is vital that there develop within the Christian tradition the concept that Jesus' teachings lie well within the continuum of first century Jewish religious thought and practice.(65)

The above examples from Haim Cohn's analysis of the Gospel record should serve to underline the need for Christian commentary on "New Testament" scripture in general and on the Gospels in particular. The Gospels need to receive special emphasis because they contain the central affirmations of Christianity. Therefore, developing commentary to offset anti-Judaic passages is especially imperative for the Gospels. An affirmation found within the Christian canon which HaShoah calls into question is that redemption is accomplished through the death and Resurrection of Jesus of Nazareth. The historian Karl Löwith interprets the traditional Christian concept of the Resurrection as being that human history is invisibly, yet fundamentally, changed therefrom. Evil, though very much with us, has been defeated by Christ. Yet it is a Christian, Robert McAfee Brown, who poses the question which needs to be pondered and resolved: "The Messiah has come. Why is the world so evil?"(66) In his work, Meaning in History, Karl Löwith offers a rationale for Dr. Brown's question.

As a history of the world, the empirical history after Christ is qualitatively not different from the history before Christ if judged from either a strictly empirical or strictly Christian viewpoint. History is, through all the ages, a story of action and suffering, of power and pride, of sin and death.(67) ...The world is the same as it was in the time of Alaric;(68) only our means of oppression and destruction (as well as reconstruction) are considerably improved and are adorned with hypocrisy.(69)

In a world which has had a history of human suffering, Christians have traditionally affirmed that the Kingdom of G-d was initiated through the life, death, and Resurrection of Jesus. This faith statement is now largely spiritualized to mean that the Kingdom exists on a non-historical level, namely, within the hearts of those who believe. The great Jewish scholar Martin Buber(70) once wrote that the Christian is one who displays much courage and hope in saying that the Kingdom of G-d is already in progress. An example of contemporary Roman Catholic belief on the merit of suffering is found in Christ Among Us. According to this modern cathechism, "Joy and hope are natural, then, to true followers of Christ. We know that whatever we suffer now will someday end in the joy of heaven with our glorified Savior.(71) Christ showed us that suffering has great power to spread love in the world, to bring ourselves and others to heaven."(72) Though these thoughts are applicable to certain human situations, I submit that the Holocaust of the Jewish people stands far outside this perception of suffering. The thought of Thomas A. Idinopulos is noteworthy here.

I myself cannot read Night(73) without feeling that the time has long since past when one could accept the cross as the symbol of healing through sacrifice, of restoring the order of things by the shedding of innocent blood ....What Wiesel's story teaches me is that if God and man wait to be reconciled and the world be made whole by the blood of a young innocent Jew in the twentieth century as in the first century, perhaps salvation isn't worth the cost. Dostoevsky understood this when in The Brothers Karamozov he had Ivan say to his younger brother Alyosha, 'I renounce the higher harmony altogether. It's not worth the tears of ... one tortured child....'(74)

What moral advance was made by the destruction of one Jew in the first century?, for it is obvious the world has made no moral progress following the destruction of six million Jews in the twentieth century. A. Roy Eckardt does not believe that the terror of the Holocaust can be redeemed by any past event, no matter how holy and divine.(75) Instead, Eckardt looks to a future event as the only possible source of redemption for HaShoah. In her work, Faith and Fratricide, Rosemary Ruether similarly suggests that Christology reinterpret the Christ-event from past and present salvation to future victory.(76) Yet how can one place the terror and suffering of Jewish children in the schema of a forward-looking theodicy?(77) What goodness inherent in heaven can atone for such unwarranted pain? I submit that ultimately no event, on any plane, can redeem the suffering that was the Holocaust -- neither the creation of the political State of Israel nor the attainment of a distant heaven! Interpretation of the Christ-event in the context of a future meaning is not only unacceptable to orthodox Christian doctrine; it also places unfounded emphasis upon a future "setting all things right" event. The meaning of human history and particularly free will are thus sacrificed for ultimate "neatness". Let us explain this thought in more detail. Man has been given freedom of will, freedom to accept or reject G-d himself. The sanctity of free will is the only concrete theological reason I can see to explain the Holocaust.(78) G-d endowed man with intelligence to use freely in making decisions. Man chose, in turn, to engineer and operate the concentration camp system. G-d did not interrupt the Nazi Final Solution to end the evil and set things right in the name of justice and mercy. The innocent were allowed to perish by the thousands day after day. Why then do we continue to hope for G-d to step in at the terminus of time and convert all the evil that occurred throughout the centuries into goodness and glory? The freedom of will helps to make the evil of the past and present understandable and even bearable. To abolish the sanctity of that freedom at the eschaton, the end of time, is to render human history and human suffering meaningless.

As mentioned previously, the Church has affirmed that the Resurrection of Jesus ushered in the Kingdom of G-d. For Christians, Jesus fulfilled Jewish messianic hopes. To assert that Jesus was the Messiah, the

Christ,(79) is to make him appear unbelievable to Jews. Jewish messianism of the first century centered about the theme of an <u>overtly</u> <u>different</u> <u>age</u> brought about on earth with the Messiah serving as the symbol for that epoch. The Messiah would be one who would deliver the people and usher in the messianic age. This age would be an era of peace and no suffering. In mainline Jewish tradition, the Messiah is a human being who will sit in the throne of David. The Messiah is not a spiritual concept to Jews, but is thought of in terms of an historical reality. Following the Endlösung, and Martin Buber to the contrary, I submit that it requires more fortitude to say that, though the Kingdom of G-d is not yet upon us, I will work to make my own part of the world a better place in which to live. Any rethinking of the traditional Christian concepts of suffering and redemption would do well to follow the directive of Irving Greenberg: "No statement, theological or otherwise, should be made that would not be credible in the presence of burning children."(80) It is noteworthy that the Christian concept of redemption is "not a process but an 'event'."(81) Redemption is thought not to occur through the workings of time and history but rather through an identifiable microcosm of history, in effect, a specific event. Christianity might consider redemption and salvation in the framework of <u>Becoming</u>. "The sacred <u>is</u> not, but has to be brought into being as the result of someone's action or behavior."(82) If Christianity were to consider salvation as a <u>process</u>, apocalypticism and the "flight from history" would be exchanged for historical responsibility. As in the Jewish perspective, redemption would then be brought about by individual effort over time. Social awareness and involvement would be invested with greater importance.

In light of the revelation provided by HaShoah, it should be apparent to Christians that there is no legitimate mission to the Jews. Rather, the task of the Church today is to affirm the Christian faith while simultaneously maintaining the integrity and validity of the Jewish people. <u>This</u> <u>task</u> <u>constitutes</u> <u>the</u> <u>essential</u> <u>challenge</u> <u>for</u> <u>post-Holocaust</u> <u>Christianity</u>. The Christian Church has traditionally stated its theological claim to the Truth in a way that disparages and negates Judaism as a religious reality. Yet why must the Jews of all time be cast in derogatory imagery and symbolism that add nothing to the Christian message? One should perhaps examine the vital signs of a religion which is so unresponsive to the practical consequences of its own symbolism upon fellow human beings and religious brethren in particular. Christian proselytizing directed towards the Jews amounts to telling the Jews: You can be true to your Jewishness only by accepting Jesus of Nazareth as the Christ, the awaited Messiah. It should be obvious that for a Jew to do so, he would no longer be a Jew. Christian attempts at converting Jews serve only to call the Christian foundation into question.(83) If a Jew is to forsake his Judaism, and if Judaism is the root of Christianity, then somehow the very foundation of Christian tradition is unstable. The West German Christian theologian Rudolf Pfisterer wonders what difference there is between putting Jews into ovens and striking at the heart of their religious identity through missionizing. The Christian claim inherent in proselytizing -- that only through Christ can one hope to experience G-d -- allows no viable religious alternatives to Christianity. Extrapolated, this stance results in a Christian universalism which is intolerant of religious identity and differences in human mythic experience and insight. How can the Church proclaim the Christian truth without neutralizng Jewish validity or making mention of proselytizing? Christians might consider the following statement as a possible vehicle to convey their own religious truth in a manner not detrimental to Judaism. <u>Christianity provides the possibility for people to live the way G-d wants them to; Christianity brings gentiles to observance of the Noahide commandments.</u>(84) For Christians to make even the seemingly innocuous affirmation that Jesus was a step in the long revelatory process of Israel is to imply that the Jewish community misread or completely overlooked Jesus as a major focal point in the divine-human encounter.

If, as we are assuming, Auschwitz is revelation for Christianity; then out of this occurrence must emerge further unfolding of the nature of G-d. Revelation is, after all, the manner by which Deity unveils himself to people.(85) What sort of G-d comes forth from the ashes of HaShoah? What can the Christian affirm about G-d in the wake of Buchenwald and Babi Yar?(86) Dr. Alice L. Eckhardt focuses these G-d-related issues in her question, "Can a theology of a responsive and saving God survive the test of the Holocaust?"(87) By way of answer to Professor Eckhardt's inquiry, the Roman Catholic theologian Gregory G. Baum "finds he must reject the traditional concepts of providence, omniscience, and omnipotence."(88) Baum's evaluation of the post-Holocaust role of Deity is that "God's power over the world is not the miraculous action by which he makes things happen as he pleases, but the redemptive action by which he enables men to deal with their own problems."(89), and by which He calls people to "resist evil and find ways of conquering it."(90) It has been suggested by A. Roy Eckardt that G-d should suffer with His people because the "ultimate responsibility for evil in the world is God's, for the simple reason that it is he who created the world and it is he who permits monstrous suffering to take place."(91) Like Eckardt, Franklin Sherman contends that the "suffering God" is the motif which directly confronts the Holocaust problematic.(92) That G-d suffers with His people implies that He is loving and concerned for His human creations on earth. Because Auschwitz happened, G-d's ability and desire to alter conditions resulting in human suffering may best be considered as limited or restrained. Divine restraint evidently follows from the sanctity of man's free will. The Holocaust strongly suggests that temporal history is not synonymous with G-d's desires for mankind. Teleology(93) within the historical plane may be said to be provided by man and not be G-d after the Death Camps. That is, if historical motion is from the present (point A) to some point in the future (point B), traditional Christian theology held that G-d determined the location of point B. Post-Holocaust Christian theology will have to consider the possibility that point B in the distant future is determined by the actions of man. G-d would then be seen as sustaining human effort in a direction that man would chart for himself. In this historical model, free will would be intact throughout time and not be discarded at the end of history. If the deaths of six million Jews were allowed because of the apparent sanctity of free will, why should G-d at the eschaton declare free will to be abolished? How could G-d then be a G-d of goodness, justice, and mercy?

The nature of G-d as developed herein argues strongly for historical responsibility on the part of the Christian community. Historical responsibility involves foremost the conviction that particular events in time and space are meaningful. It is this conviction which liberal Protestantism often rejects. The particular history and identity of any religious community are rejected in favor of a spiritual universalism. In the liberal Christian mind, the integrity of the Jewish people as a distinctive people is disavowed.(94) The Jewish people is spiritualized into Judaism. A multi-dimensional people is consigned to the status of a religion. Yet the Holocaust graphically demonstrated that the Jewish people is a neither a religion nor a spiritual concept. The Jewish people does not equal Judaism. HaShoah must reveal to the liberal Christian that the Jewish people is a concrete, specific historical reality whose members bleed! It should be recalled that the Nazis and their supporters exterminated observant Jews, Reform Jews, Jewish atheists, and Jews who converted to Christianity. Religion in the liberal Christian sense of the word was therefore not the primary delineator of Jewish people in the Nazi mentality. The spiritual religion espoused by liberal Christianity does not command its adherents to be outwardly separate from the culture in which they live. If the Holocaust reveals anything to Christianity, it should convey the message that Christians, like Jews, are called by G-d to be a separate community.(95) Christianity should be the commitment of a particular people in this world, not a spiritual religion with focus upon another world.

Let us now begin to assemble suggestions which may make a measurable difference in Christian attitudes towards Jews, and consequently, in Jewish attitudes towards Christians. Education is a significant component of any effort to effect attitudinal changes. Beginning at the level of the clergy, the inclusion of Judaic Studies Departments in Christian seminaries along with courses specifically treating the Holocaust might go far in sensitizing people going into the ministry to the impact of Christian symbolism and teaching upon today's Jews. There is also urgent need for re-evaluation and update of Protestant and Catholic teaching materials regarding Judaism and Jewish people.(96) A cross-section of religious teaching materials used in American Sunday schools and adult education classes was documented to contain negative images of Jews and Judaism as late as 1972.(97) Following HaShoah, basic tools of learning such as the theological dictionaries should reflect heightened Christian sensitivity towards Jews. An example of what one such dictionary includes under the heading of "Judaism" should demonstrate the type of misconception in need of alteration.

> The bulk of religious Jews have accommodated themselves to a greater or lesser extent to the world in which they live. ...It is probable that the majority of Jews are effectively atheist, whether they keep up a link with the synagogue or not.(98)

36

It must be remembered that in America, atheism is popularly associated with communism. The attitudes of the faculty members of Christian seminaries are also in need of revision regarding Jews. George Wesley Buchanan, a seminary professor of "New Testament", explains the suffering of the Jewish people throughout history in the following manner.

> Saboteurs are generally not welcomed by the citizens of a country, so it is not surprising that a people religiously dedicated to international sabotage should have a long history of persecution.(99)

Dr. Buchanan expressed these thoughts about Jews in 1971 in the journal Religion in Life. His viewpoint warrants no comment.

Another area requiring Christian reconsideration involves the application of the word new in theological context. The part of the Christian bible referred to as the "New Testament" might be rendered as Apostolic Writings,(100) Pauline Epistles, or Christian canon. The terms old and new, when applied to sacred writings, imply that the new has somehow surpassed or fulfilled the old. Also in need of reevaluation are the constructs Old and New Israel. New Israel is the title the Church took for her own in the early centuries of the common era. New Israel, used as a synonym for the Church, implies that Jewish validity as a religious reality is gone.

The widespread incorporation of a Holocaust Remembrance Service into the Church liturgical calendar would be a clear signal of Christian awareness of and response to Jewish suffering.(101) The Eastern Pennsylvania Conference of the United Methodist church is noteworty in this regard. The conference adopted a resolution in June, 1978 to set aside a Sunday in April to reflect upon the significance of the "Martyrdom of Six Million Jews in Europe from 1933 to 1945..."(102) According to Franklin H. Littell, there are currently two hundred churches nationwide which conduct a Yom HaShoah Remembrance Service.(103)

An action which necessarily involves the cooperation of the Roman Catholic hierarchy also may help assure the Jewish community that Christians hear the anguish of HaShoah. The action for which I am calling is the excommunication of Adolf Hitler from the Roman Catholic church.(104) Though it has been argued that

Hitler was not a practicing Catholic,(105) the Roman Catholic church to this day excommunicates relatively insignificant Catholic persons who do not conform to church regulations. The infractions which can be met with excommunication include remarriage after civil divorce. From the excommunication of Hitler would emerge an unclouded statement of concern for the Jews of Europe who died in the Final Solution.

Foremost among the range of potential Christian responses to the Holocaust must be the commitment to effect change in the liturgy at the level of the individual church. Offsetting commentary on the Christian canon, for example, will be given the special emphasis of religious sanction if presented in the context of the worship service.(106) When experienced directly in the framework of the church service, offsetting commentary, a Holocaust Remembrance Service, and historically-aware religious education constitute the beginnings of Christian reorientation born of the revelation of Auschwitz.

NOTES

CHAPTER II

THE HOLOCAUST
AS IT MIGHT AFFECT CHRISTIAN THEOLOGY

1. The use of the designation <u>Christian Church</u> in this chapter is not to imply that <u>Christianity</u> is a monolithic phenomenon. The rich variety within the Christian tradition is found in the following listing which has no pretense of being complete: Assemblies of God, Southern Baptist, Christian Science, Church of Jesus Christ of Latter-Day Saints (Mormon), Church of the Nazarene, Eastern Orthodox Catholic church in America, Episcopal church, Society of Friends (insensitively referred to as Quaker), Lutheran church, Mennonite church, Jehovah's Witnesses, United Methodist church, United Presbyterian church, Reformed Church of America, Roman Catholic church, Salvation Army, and United Church of Christ. Obviously there is a wide range of viewpoint and specific faith affirmations among the different church bodies comprising what I call Christian Church. However, there is some commonality among these denominations and splinter churches. It is on the basis of this commonality of tradition and vision that I feel I can allude to such an entity as the Christian Church.

2. It should be stressed that there exists a great plurality of viewpoint among the Christian scholars and theologians pondering the meaning of the Holocaust. Despite that the scholars are focusing upon the same event, their conclusions sometimes vary diametrically.

3. Dr. Franklin H. Littell is professor of religion at Temple University in Philadelphia. A United Methodist clergyman and church historian, Professor Littell's abiding interest as expressed by his writing is the Church Struggle in Nazi Germany and the Holocaust. Dr. Littell is honorary chairman of the National Institute on the Holocaust and has been the primary organizer of many major Holocaust conferences. He is also a member of the United States Holocaust Memorial Council.

4. Roy Eckardt is professor in and chairman of the Department of Religion at Lehigh University in

Bethlehem, Pennsylvania. Dr. Eckardt, a United Methodist scholar, is the author of many books and articles on the relationship of Jews and Christians.

5. Reverend John T. Pawlikowski, a Roman Catholic priest of the Order of the Servants of Mary, is chairman of the Department of Historical and Doctrinal Studies and associate professor at Catholic Theological Union in Chicago. Father Pawlikowski defines himself to be a social ethicist.

6. Rosemary Radford Ruether teaches theology at Garrett-Evangelical Seminary in Evanston, Illinois. Dr. Ruether is Roman Catholic.

7. Harry James Cargas is professor in both the Department of Literature and Language and the Department of Religion at Webster University in St. Louis. He describes himself as a post-Auschwitz Catholic. Dr. Cargas has been appointed to the United States Holocaust Memorial Council. His work is strongly influenced by the thought and experience of Elie Wiesel. Professor Cargas writes from the heart as well as the mind.

8. For additional information on official Church statements on Jewish-Christian relationship and anti-Semitism, see Michael B. McGarry, *Christology after Auschwitz*. Father McGarry is a Paulist priest. An example of an official Church statement on the Jewish people is Article Four of the "Declaration on the Relation of the Church to Non-Christian Religions" issued by the Second Vatican Council of the Roman Catholic church.

9. *Laity level* refers to the many church congregations and parishes and the individual Christians of which these are comprised. Technically, laity refers to all persons who are not clergy.

10. *Endlösung* is part of the German Nazi phrase, *Endlösung der Judenfrage*, "The Final Solution to the Jewish Question". According to historian Lucy S. Dawidowicz, the term *Jewish Question* was first used during the Enlightenment period of the eighteenth century in Western Europe. The Jewish Question involved the unusual persistence of the Jews to remain a coherent and identifiable people despite the growing social homogeneity of the new nation-states. What should be done, the new political nationalisms wanted to know, with a group of people that did not willingly submerge itself

40

into the population-in-general. The Nazi Final Solution to this two hundred fifty year-old question was but one of many solutions proposed over the years.

11. The word dis-orienting is used specifically to challenge the notion that the Holocaust was a re-orienting event. Rather than provide a new moral and theological compass, the Holocaust has caused us to drift without the benefit of time-worn moral rudders. A. Roy Eckardt speaks of the Holocaust being metanoia, the "climactic turning-around of the entire world." "Is the Holocaust Unique?," Worldview 17(1974):35. Professor Eckardt seems to see HaShoah as being an event which indeed does provide direction for our culture and for Christianity in particular.

12. The mobile killing units that followed the German armies into the Soviet Union were called Einsatzgruppen. Ernst Biberstein, an officer in Einsatzgruppe C, had become a Protestant pastor in 1924. For additional personal history of Ernst Biberstein, see Raul Hilberg, The Destruction of the European Jews, pp. 188-89.

13. The observation of Christian involvement with American blacks and Native Americans was borrowed from Robert E. Willis, "Confessing God After Auschwitz: A Challenge for Christianity," Cross Currents 28(1978): 274. Dr. Willis, a United Presbyterian minister, is professor of religion at Hamline University in Saint Paul, Minnesota.

14. Examples of anti-Judaic Christian practice include the First Crusade of 1096, the Third and Fourth Lateran Council decisions of 1179 and 1215, and the Spanish Inquisition of the late fifteenth century.

Jules M. Isaac (1877-1963), a French historian, had a book titled Jesus et Israel (Jesus and Israel) published in 1948. Isaac's work demonstrated in clear fashion how closely the contempt for the Jewish people and the Jewish religion were linked to Christian teaching and preaching from the "New Testament". His writing had great influence on the decision to introduce a statement on relations with the Jews at the Second Vatican Council that ended in 1965. See also, Jules M. Isaac, The Teaching of Contempt. Jules Isaac was Jewish.

Dr. Richard L. Rubenstein, in a speech delivered at the Eighth Annual Philadelphia Conference on the Holocaust held in October, 1982, postulated that Christianity used specifically religious language to discredit Jews and Judaism because the Church had no sociological or political language to do so. Professor Rubenstein teaches in the Department of Religion at Florida State University in Tallahassee, Florida.

15. Certainly other elements were necessary to produce such a system as the National Socialists developed in addition to the attitudes deriving from anti-Judaic Christian teaching. To postulate direct causal relationship between those anti-Judaic teachings and Auschwitz implies an historical fatalism which is not conducive to meaningful interpretation of events. One must be wary of placing guilt at the collective Christian doorstep. As Richard Rubenstein has noted, guilt has a way of being transposed into hatred of the perceived causal agent, which in the instance of HaShoah, is the Jews. Contrition for the Holocaust can legitimately begin only within the hearts and minds of concerned Christians by means of their own will. Guilt cannot be imposed; only issues, problems, and solutions exposed.

16. Negative images of the Jew deriving from Christian teaching include: "Christ-killer", "devil incarnate", "materialistic as opposed to spiritual", "stiff-necked and stubborn", "spiritually blind to the awaited Messiah", and "deserving of divine punishment". For instance, in the Good Friday services at many churches there is recitation from the Gospels wherein responsibility for the Crucifixion of Jesus is laid upon the Jewish people. The Gospel account reads as if the Jews forced the Roman authorities into reluctantly executing Jesus.

17. Precisely because the Church deals with the ultimates in human experience, its power to shape unconscious attitudes is so strong. The Cross, in effect, is a more powerful symbol than the American flag. That is, patriotism and nationalism do not evoke the same depth of feeling and attendant attitudes as does religious faith, which deals with such questions as, "What happens to me when I die?" and "What is the meaning of life?" Picture a Cross and an American flag, if you will, and ask yourself which of the two evokes the more emotion.

Language is a system comprised of symbols, or words. Such word-symbols, in psychological terms, have two levels at which they are comprehended. MIT psychologist Noam Chomsky defined those two levels to be <u>surface structure</u> and <u>deep structure</u>. In Chomskian terms, the American flag might be understood to operate as a symbol on the surface level, while the Cross evokes response and comprehension at the deep structure level. Other symbols in addition to words could also be put in surface/deep structure terms.

18. Common era is a term used by non-Christians to refer to the time popularly known as A.D.

19. For further explanation of this traditional Christian historical model, see A. Roy Eckardt, "Christians and Jews: Along a Theological Frontier," <u>Encounter</u> 40(1979): 90-92, 96; and Alan T. Davies, "Response to Irving Greenberg," in <u>Auschwitz: Beginning of a new Era?</u> ed. Eva Marie Fleischner, pp. 61-62. Alan T. Davies is professor of Religious Studies at the University of Toronto. He has served as a minister of the United Church of Canada.

20. Eckardt, "Christians and Jews," p. 91.

21. See John J. Hick, <u>Evil and the God of Love</u>, pp. 297, 397-98 for a modern Christian treatment of theodicy. <u>Theodicy</u>, a term probably coined by the German philosopher Gottfried Leibnitz in his work <u>Theodicy</u> (1710), refers to the effort to reconcile an <u>all-good</u> and <u>all-powerful</u> G-d with the moral and physical evil in the world. <u>Theodicy</u> is a synthesis of two Greek words that mean "deity" and "justice". John Hick stands among many Christian theologians who have wrestled with the problem of evil and G-d. Saint Augustine (Bishop of Hippo in Algeria; 354-430 C.E.) looked back to the Fall of Man to discern the reason for evil in the world. See John H. Hick, ed., <u>Classical and Contemporary Readings in Philosophy</u>, p. 19 for Augustine's understanding of G-d and evil quoted from his <u>Confessions and Enchiridion</u>. Irenaeus, a church father from the second century of the common era, found justification for evil in the infinite good which G-d will bring out of human history in the future. Similar to Irenaeus, Hick resolves evil by appealing to the good that may come at the eschaton, the end of days.

22. <u>Ibid.</u>, p. 398.

23. See Deut. 5:33 and Josh. 1:8 for two expressions of the deuteronomic formula. The book of Job offers an offsetting interpretation of evil. Job, who was a righteous man, has much evil befall him. The

book of Job teaches that what G-d decides to do is not easily understood by human beings. Man is not necessarily rewarded in this life for righteousness.

24. The Darmstadt Conference is mentioned in Eckardt, "Christians and Jews," pp. 98-99. The Evangelical church council has since revised its stance on the Jews.

25. The <u>divine-human encounter</u> is a term often used to mean revelation.

26. Golgotha was the hill outside Jerusalem on which Jesus was crucified.

27. A. Roy Eckardt, "The Recantation of the Covenent?," in <u>Confronting the Holocaust</u>, eds. Irving Greenberg and Alvin H. Rosenfeld, p. 163. Jürgen Moltmann is a German theologian at the University of Tübingen. See Jürgen Moltmann, <u>The Crucified God</u> for his best-known work.

28. Revelation at Sinai refers to G-d giving the Jewish people the Torah and the Oral Law on Mount Sinai. <u>Torah</u> is derived from the root word ירה, "to teach"; and therefore, means "teaching, doctrine, or instruction". Torah refers specifically to the Pentateuch as opposed to the rest of the Tanach. The Pentateuch is composed of the five books of Moses -- Genesis, Exodus, Leviticus, Numbers, and Deuteronomy. <u>Tanach</u> is an acronym for the entire Hebrew Bible, which includes the Torah, the Prophets, and the Writings. It should be emphasized that <u>Torah</u> should not be translated as "Law", because Law mistakenly connotes rigid legalism. The Jewish code of ethics, <u>Halacha</u>, which is derived from the Torah, is often defined or translated as "Law". <u>Halacha</u> actually means "pathway, road, or way of life". The Hebrew word <u>derech</u>, "road", is associated with Halacha.

Oral Law refers to information imparted to Moses on Mount Sinai which was to be used to further interpret the Torah. The Oral Law was not codified (written down) initially in order to prevent it from becoming ossified. It was finally written in what is called the <u>Talmud</u> during the beginning of the common era to insure that it would not be lost. The tenuous political situation in Palestine accounts for this codification. Despite being in written form, the Talmud did not become outdated because of the tradition of ongoing commentary and constant re-interpretation.

Commentary in the Jewish tradition is given almost as much authority as the scriptures.

29. Dr. Brown is professor of theology and ethics at the Pacific School of Religion. He is also a member of the United States Holocaust Memorial Council.

30. The burning bush reference comes from the third chapter of Exodus. Through the burning bush, G-d revealed himself to Moses. Moses was told to return to Egypt to help the Jewish people leave the country. The burning bush is an example of theopany.

31. <u>Kerygma</u> refers to the primitive Gospel message. The term was used by C. H. Dodd in his discussion of the Gospel published in 1936.

32. Harry James Cargas, "World Literature and the Holocaust," <u>Christian Century</u> 96(1979): 1125.

33. Eckardt, "Christians and Jews," p. 101.

34. Father Hans Küng is a prominent European Roman Catholic theologian regarded to be quite liberal and radical in Catholic circles. His ideas were heard in a lecture he delivered at Gettysburg College, Gettysburg, Pennsylvania on 16 November 1981.

35. Harry James Cargas, "A Post-Auschwitz Catholic," <u>Christian Century</u> 95(1978): 1063.

36. Franklin H. Littell, <u>The Crucifixion of the Jews</u>, p. 65.

37. Thomas A. Idinopulos and Roy Bowen Ward, "Is Christology Inherently Anti-Semitic? A Critical Review of Rosemary Ruether's <u>Faith and Fratricide</u>," <u>Journal of the American Academy of Religion</u> 45(1977): 200. Dr. Idinopulos, a Christian, is professor of religion at Miami University of Ohio in Oxford, Ohio. He teaches in the areas of philosophical theology, religion and literature, and modern Jewish thought. Dr. Ward is chairman of the Department of Religion at Miami University of Ohio. His focus is early Christianity.

38. <u>Ibid</u>., p. 200.

39. An example of the Christian emphasis on the next world and upon only spiritual things comes by way of the frequently heard call for pastors to "stick to

the Gospel" in sermons and homilies. This call comes from congregations which do not want to hear the Christian message applied to such social and moral issues as nuclear weapons, hunger, poverty, unemployment, and abortion.

40. Sub ratione peccati was a phrase used by John T. Pawlikowski, "The Holocaust as Rational Event," Reconstructionist 40(1974): 12.

41. Friedrich Heer, God's First Love, p. 406.

42. Deus ex machina is derived from the Greek theos ek mekhanes. Translated form the New Latin, the phrase becomes "god from a machine". A deity in Greek and Roman drama was brought onstage by machinery to intervene in a difficult situation.

43. Miracle is usually understood in terms of G-d altering the laws of nature as we know them to effect a particular result in human history.

44. Deity, which means Divinity or G-d, is derived from the Latin word deus.

45. Dietrich Bonhoeffer was a German Protestant clergyman who was an outspoken critic of National Socialism. He was arrested in 1943 and imprisoned by the Nazis. Bonhoeffer was hanged in 1945. See Dietrich Bonhoeffer, Prisoner for God.

46. Privately in this sense means that one's life should not be public ostentation regarding one's relationship with G-d.

47. The concept of the Holocaust constituting a new revelation, that is, a further unfolding of the G-d-human interchange, is found in Eckardt, "Recantation of the Covenant?," p. 163. Franklin H. Littell visualizes the Holocaust to be an "alpine event" for Christians. He believes that the "Holocaust and the restoration of Israel are basic events in Christian history -- of the same order as the Exodus, Sinai, the fall of Rome." "Christendom, Holocaust, and Israel: The Importance for Christians of Recent Major Events in Jewish History," Journal of Ecumenical Studies 10(1973): 469-97. Littell's mention of the restoration of Israel refers to the establishment of the State of Israel in 1948.

In a similar vein, Elwyn A. Smith asserts that "the question whether Christianity is to remember the holocaust or dismiss it is a question of the ability and the right of Christianity to survive in a form in any way conformable to the Scripture." "The Christian Meaning of the Holocaust," Journal of Ecumenical Studies 6(1969): 422.

In the view of these three scholars, it is imperative that the Holocaust become a source of change and learning within the Christian community.

48. The theological anchor metaphor was borrowed from Robert E. Willis, "Christian Theology after Auschwitz," Journal of Ecumenical Studies 12(1975): 510.

49. Apostolic Writings refer to the Gospels -- Matthew, Mark, Luke, and John. The Letters of Paul include such "New Testament" books as Corinthians, Romans, and Galatians.

50. Jewish houses of worship include shuls, synagogues and temples. Shuls are Orthodox places of worship. Synagogues are usually Conservative, though they may also be Orthodox. Temples are usually Reform houses of worship.

51. See Eliezer Berkovits, Faith after the Holocaust, p. 47.

52. A more virulent version of the triumphalist claim asserts that the Jews purposefully rejected Jesus as the awaited Messiah. Another term used for the triumphalist claim is supersessionist myth.

53. Covenant refers to the special relationship which exists between G-d and the Jewish people embodied in the biblical passage: I (G-d) will take you to be my people, and I will be your G-d.

54. Communists, for example, were killed by the Nazis for political reasons. Mentally and physically handicapped individuals were murdered in the euthanasia program.

55. Christianity has traditionally viewed the destruction of the Temple in Jerusalem as a sign that G-d rescinded any special relationship with the Jewish people.

56. Eva Marie Fleischner, "The Crucial Importance of the Holocaust for Christians," Engage/Social Action, December 1976, p. 32.

57. Shakespeare's Merchant of Venice, for example, has been called anti-Semitic, especially in the character of Shylock.

58. Robert E. Willis argues that "the career of anti-semitism within the church could have been deflected or neutralized somewhat if certain other passages in the Christian scripture had been opposed to those that cast aspersion on 'the Jews'. "Confessing God," p. 276.

59. Rashi is an acronym of Rabbi Shlomo Yitchaki (1040-1105), who lived in Troyes, France. His commentary is considered the basic Biblical commentary, essential for understanding the Torah.

60. Rambam is an acronym referring to Moses Mainmonides (1135-1204). His scholarship embraced all Biblical and rabbinic literature as well as the science and philosophy of his day. He was also an accomplished physician.

61. Ramban is an acronym referring to Nachmanides (1195-1270). Ramban was a talmudic scholar and theologian who also studied philosophy and science.

62. Liturgy refers to the combination of hymns and scriptural readings which make up the worship service.

63. Haim Cohn is Supreme Court Justice in Israel and has represented Israel on the United Nations Commission on Human Rights. He is editor of Jewish Law in Ancient and Modern Israel along with numerous scholarly books and articles. He studied philosophy and Semitic languages at the University of Munich, rabbinical studies in Israel, and law in Germany. He graduated from the Palestine Government Law School in 1937. From 1937-48, Mr. Justice Cohn was an attorney in Jerusalem. He has served as Israeli State Attorney, Director-General of the Ministry of Justice, and Attorney-General of Israel. He has also held the cabinet-level post of Minister of Justice. Recently, Cohn was elected to the Board of Governors of the International Institute of Human Rights in Strasbourg, France. He is

a lecturer on the History of Penal Law, Penal Philosophy, and Jurisprudence at the university level in Israel.

    64. Jesus' alleged disagreement with the Pharisees concerning healing on the Sabbath is found in Matt. 12:9-14. By way of background, the Pharisees were one of several Jewish religious groups extant in Palestine in the first century. Included among the other Jewish religious groups were the Sadducees, Essenes, and Zealots. The Pharisees were willing to apply the teachings of the Torah to situations in contemporary life, thereby re-interpreting and updating the scripture. As a group, the Pharisees were revered by the general Jewish population of Palestine. It was Pharisaic teaching which eventually grew into the rabbinic Judaism which exists today.

    The scriptural injunction against work on the Sabbath, which is the crux of the issue surrounding Matt. 12:9-14, is found in Exod. 20:8-11. See Samson Raphael Hirsch, trans., The Pentateuch. The meaning behind the mitzvah, "commandment", found in Exod. 20:8-11 is for man to dedicate one day every week to G-d. On this one day, man was to refrain from "every activity which signifies human power over nature." Isidor Grunfeld, The Sabbath, p. 27. "On this day we (Jews) renounce every exercise of intelligent, purposeful control over natural objects and forces, we cease from every act of human power, in order to proclaim God as the Source of all power. By refraining from human creating, the Jew pays silent homage to the Creator." Ibid., p. 28. The parentheses here are my own.

    The notion of simply not doing work on the Sabbath is misleading because work is popularly thought of as physical labor. The Hebrew word in the Bible that is translated as "work" is melakhah. Rather than physical labor, however, melakhah connotes "'the realization of an intelligent purpose by practical skill.'" Ibid. Though healing the sick and dying on the Sabbath would indeed constitute the use of skill to achieve intelligent purpose, there exists a specific rabbinic injunction (pickuach nefesh) which demands that a Jew do what is necessary to relieve pain and illness on the Sabbath. Thus, the Pharisees and Jesus were not in tension on this issue.

    65. See John T. Pawlikowski, Christ in the Light of Christian Jewish Dialogue. The main part of this volume offers a new model for the relationship between

Christology and Judaism rooted in an understanding of Jesus' link with the Pharisees.

It should be noted that the famous Jewish teacher Hillel (30 B.C.E. to 10 C.E.) advanced many ideas similar to those of Jesus. Therefore, there was not the degree of novelty in Jesus' teachings which the Church claims.

66. Robert McAfee Brown, "The Holocaust: The Crisis of Indifference." <u>Conservative Judaism</u> 31(1976-1977): 19.

67. Karl Löwith, <u>Meaning in History</u>, p. 190.

68. Alaric was the conqueror of Rome (410 C.E.).

69. Löwith, <u>Meaning in History</u>, p. 191.

70. Martin Buber (1878-1965) is best known for his revival of Hasidism, a mystical movement which swept East European Jewry in the eighteenth and nineteenth centuries. Professor Buber taught philosophy from 1938-1951 at Hebrew University in Jerusalem. He was a Zionist leader and thinker.

71. Anthony J. Wilhelm, <u>Christ Among Us</u>, p. 119.

72. <u>Ibid</u>., p. 118.

73. In his work <u>Night</u>, Elie Wiesel describes his personal experiences in Auschwitz. The book is far more than an autobiographical or historical account; it is haunting, profound prose.

74. Thomas A. Idinopulos, "Christianity and the Holocaust," <u>Cross Currents</u> 28(1978): 265. A. Roy Eckardt also sees problems with the idea of redemption through suffering after the Holocaust event. For Eckardt, in the wake of history in general and Auschwitz in particular, "a question mark is nailed to the Cross as the reputedly determinative symbol of redemptive suffering." "Jews and Christians," p. 102.

75. Eckardt, "Jews and Christians," p. 125.

76. This interpretation of Ruether was borrowed from Idinopulos and Ward, "Is Christology Anti-Semitic?," p. 205.

77. Hans O. Tiefel also disagrees with a forward-looking theodicy. "But, of course, the sufferings of the Holocaust are irretrievable, and the suggestion that they may work toward some greater good, that those who died were means toward a better end, is abhorrent." "Holocaust Interpretations and Religious Assumptions," Judaism 25(1976): 141. Professor Tiefel teaches religion at William and Mary College.

78. I submit that Christians will be hard pressed to complete the statement: "Theologically, the Holocaust occurred because ..." in a way not disparaging to the Jewish victims.

79. The word Christ comes from the Greek word Christos. Christos was the Greek equivalent for the Hebrew word for Messiah. Messiah means "the anointed one", and was applied to such figures as the Babylonian king, Cyrus.

80. Irving Greenberg, "Judaism and Christianity after the Holocaust," Journal of Ecumenical Studies 12(1975): 529. Irving Greenberg (1933-) is an American Orthodox rabbi and educator. Born in Brooklyn, New York, Greenberg is a leading exponent of the Musar Movement. This movement is dedicated to the education of the individual Jew toward strict ethical behavior in the spirit of halacha (way of life). For additional information on the Musar Movement, see Lester Samuel Eckman, The History of the Musar Movement 1840-1945.

81. Berkovits, Faith after the Holocaust, p. 58. Rabbi Berkovits (1900-) is an Orthodox rabbi and theologian. Born in Transylvania, Europe, he is a modern proponent of Orthodoxy and Zionism.

82. Ibid., p. 59.

83. Some of the ideas expressed herein are borrowed from Frank E. Talmadge, "Christian Theology and the Holocaust," Commentary 60(1975): 72.

84. In Jewish thought, "the seven Noahide commandments are universally binding and all men who fulfill them will be recognized by God and share in the redemption to come." W. Richard Comstock et al., eds., Religion and Man, p. 532. The Noahide commandments are found in the ninth chapter of Genesis, which also includes the broader theme of G-d's covenant with Noah.

85. Revelation is the manner by which G-d reveals Himself to man according to orthodox Christian and Orthodox Jewish thought.

86. In 1941, there were mass shootings of Jews at Babi Yar. Babi Yar is a ravine located outside Kiev in the Ukraine area of Russia. Translated from the Russian, <u>Babi Yar</u> means "grandmother's gulch or ravine". The ignominy of this site was recorded in the poem "Babi Yar" (1961) by Yevgeny Yevtushenko.

87. Alice L. Eckhardt, "The Holocaust: Christian and Jewish Responses," <u>Journal</u> <u>of</u> <u>the</u> <u>American</u> <u>Academy</u> <u>of</u> <u>Religion</u> 42(1974): 455. Alice L. Eckardt teaches in the Department of Religion at Lehigh University in Bethlehem, Pennsylvania. She is the wife of A. Roy Eckardt.

88. <u>Ibid</u>., p. 457.

Providence: The doctrine of providence tells us that the world and our lives are not ruled by chance or fate, but by G-d.

Omniscience means that G-d knows all things.

Omnipotence means that G-d can do all things; He is all-powerful.

These definitions were taken from Everett F. Harrison, Geoffrey W. Bromiley, and Carl F. H. Henry, eds., <u>Baker's</u> <u>Dictionary</u> <u>of</u> <u>Theology</u>.

An expansion of Gregory G. Baum's thought is in order here.

> God is not provident ... in the sense that as a ruler of the world he has a master plan for human history by which he provides help for people in need, especially those who ask him for it, and by which he guides the lives of men, even while acknowledging their freedom ... (or) in which God has permitted evil and ... calculated its damaging effects and compensated for them in the final outcome .... (But) God is provident in the sense that in whatever trap man falls, a summons continues to address him and offer him life that makes him more truly human .... Gregory G. Baum,

Man Becoming, p. 242. God is omniscient (only) in the sense that there exists no human situation, however difficult, however obscure, however frightening, in which God remains silent or ... in which a summons to greater insight is not available. ... Ibid., p. 243. (Similarly), God is omnipotent (only) in the sense that there is ... no situation however destructive, in which an inner strength is not offered to man, allowing him to assume greater possession of his humanity. Ibid., p. 244.

89. Baum, Man Becoming, p. 249. Gregory Baum, a convert to Christianity from Judaism, is professor of Religious Studies at the University of Toronto.

90. Ibid., pp. 248-49.

91. Eckardt, "Is the Holocaust Unique?," p. 34.

92. Franklin Sherman, "Speaking of God after Auschwitz," Worldview 17(1974): 29. Franklin Sherman is a Lutheran theologian and professor of Christian theology at the Lutheran School of Theology in Chicago.

93. Teleology means "direction towards a goal, development".

94. The Jews, as a people, have thus far successfully resisted the modern tendency to lose their particular historical and religious contours. It is liberal thought within Christianity that sees the Jewish way of life and the Christian tradition as merely two expressions of ethical monotheism. My wife and I have personally experienced the question, "Why couldn't we send our daughter to Roman Catholic parochial school? After all, other than Jesus, Catholicism and Judaism are very much the same, aren't they?" To this seemingly innocuous inquiry, we must ask: But what of all the distinctively Jewish religious symbols and daily behaviors? The person who raised this question obviously saw both faiths as being little more than codes of ethics, which if followed, produced good people.

95. For a discussion of Christianity redefining itself as a separate community, see Littell, Crucifixion of the Jews, pp. 68-80.

96. For an examination of Christian teaching materials with respect to Jews and Judaism, see Bernhard E. Olson, Faith and Prejudice.

97. See Gerald S. Strober, Portrait of the Elder Brother.

98. Harrison, Bromiley, and Henry, eds., Dictionary of Theology, p. 302.

99. George Wesley Buchanan, "Jewish and Christian Relationships," Religion in Life 40(1971): 275. In our post-Holocaust world, Christians in general, and particularly those charged with educating pastors and priests, need to be sensitive to statements that explain Jewish suffering. Buchanan's thoughts on this issue, if not so damaging to Jewish-Christian understanding, would be ludicrous.

If I might add a parenthetical note here: Recently, the Roman Catholic community in Saint Louis reacted very strongly against a play performed in that city which was perceived to attack the fundamentals of the Catholic faith. The play was Sister Mary Ignatius Explains It All for You written by Christopher Durang. Catholics seemed to feel that the impact of the play would be to cause non-Catholics to misunderstand Catholicism. While respecting the feelings of the Saint Louis Catholic community, might not all Christians use this instance to better empathize with their Jewish brothers and sisters who have been subjected to centuries-long misrepresentation and malignment.

100. For a discussion of the term Apostolic Writings, see Harry James Cargas, A Christian Response to the Holocaust, pp. 180-81.

101. Those interested in a specific format for a Holocaust Remembrance service, see Donald W. McEvoy, A Christian Service of Holocaust Remembrance -- Yom Ha-Shoah --.

102. The United Methodist Reporter for Eastern Pennsylvania, 16 February 1979, p. 1. The resolution was adopted 15 June 1978 by the 192nd session of the Annual Conference.

103. From a speech delivered by Franklin H. Littell at the Bernhard E. Olson Scholars' Conference on the Holocaust, held in New York on 6 March 1983.

104. "Adolf Hitler was a baptized Catholic and he was never officially reprimanded by the church for his acts. His blueprint for Nazi policies, *Mein Kampf*, was never listed in Rome's *Index of Prohibited Books* -- although far less dangerous works of Jean Paul-Sartre ... did make the *Index* in this century." Harry James Cargas, "Time to Excommunicate Adolf Hitler, R.C.," *National Catholic Reporter* 16(1980): 13. *Mein Kampf* translates from the German as "my struggle".

105. See Michael Schwartz, "Are Christians Responsible?," *National Review* 32(1980): 956-58.

106. For a glimpse of the ineffectiveness of offsetting commentary on the Gospels provided in an *academic* setting, see Blu Greenberg, "Report of a Jewish Teacher," *Ecumenist* 12(1974): 84-86.

CHAPTER III

THE HOLOCAUST
AND MY CONVERSION TO JUDAISM

My religious orientation to the Holocaust is that of a Christian(1) who converted to Judaism largely as a result of my understanding of this event. I would like to stress that converting to Judaism in response to the Holocaust is not something which I advocate as an ideal or necessary reaction. Rather, it was the pathway I chose for myself. My decision-making process spanned several years, finally being translated into the conversion ceremony in May of 1981. Those several years included time during which I considered myself very much a Christian. I should add here that my wife, Nancy, also converted to Judaism in the same ceremony. She had, however, arrived at that moment for reasons different than my own. Knowledge and contemplation of the Holocaust facilitated my decision to convert to Judaism, and yet simultaneously made that choice quite difficult. I was especially concerned about the effect of my decision on the life and well-being of my two year-old daughter, Becky. My conversion to Judaism through a Reform rabbi was but the beginning of my religious development within the Jewish tradition. HaShoah has also been very much a part of my moving toward an halachic conversion.(2)

Several factors converged to bring me ultimately to my conversion to Judaism: my wife's reading and study of Jewish history and religious practice and her discussion of this reading with me, a college seminar on the Holocaust, my own study of Judaism within the context of college religious courses,(3) and a general willingness on my part to explore many options. This final element was due in part to my curiosity as a burgeoning scientist. My major course of study in college was biology. To place pertinent occurrences in a time framework, my wife and I attended college from 1973-75 and then finished our undergraduate degrees from 1977-79. The Holocaust seminar was held during the spring semester of 1979. Our conversion, as stated above, was in May of 1981.

In need of exploration and expression at this point are the primary causes for my rejecting the Christian tradition as a vital part of my life. The role that study of the Holocaust played in my intellectual and religious migration away from Christianity will be integrated appropriately. By way of background, I believe that I never had a strong affinity for, or spiritual relationship with, Jesus or the Holy Spirit. My essential religious commitment as a Christian was to G-d as the Father. Many of the theological problems that I came to see within Christianity became apparent only after I had contacted Judaism on an academic level. After college, as I continued in Holocaust study, I devoted most of my attention to HaShoah as it might affect Christian theology. My primary effort during the latter part of 1979 and the beginning of 1980 was writing a scholarly manuscript for publication.(4) It was during this period of independent research that I read and absorbed many of the works of Christian Holocaust scholars, theologians such as Franklin H. Littell and A. Roy Eckardt. These writers outline the negative impact of Christian theological affirmations upon the Jewish people throughout history in general and during the period 1933-1945 in particular. A volume by Haim Cohn, cited by A. Roy Eckardt,(5) had profound influence upon my consideration of Christianity. Cohn's work, entitled The Trial and Death of Jesus, demonstrates in convincing fashion that much of what is presented in the Gospels concerning Jewish law, custom, and practice is misleading and inaccurate. It was on the basis of such inaccuracies that Christianity built its tradition of contempt for Jews and Judaism.

I believe I am correct in stating that I initially interpreted the Holocaust as primarily a Jewish tragedy, and therefore, a Jewish problem. Such orientation was most likely the result of my reading popular books and articles on the subject prior to the Holocaust course in college. Much popular literature views the Holocaust as a single-dimension -- the physical destruction of the Jews of Europe. That the event might have import for all people and all academic disciplines is not usually presented. It was thus with a bit of surprise that I heard the professor who taught the Holocaust course say as an introductory remark to the seminar: The Holocaust was foremost a public event. The event cannot, in his estimation, be confined within specifically Jewish parameters. Perhaps as reaction against what I perceived to be, if not a denial of, then at least a minimizing of, the Jewish content of HaShoah; I sought to invest the Holocaust with Jewish meaning. This I did by attempting to make the prototypic victims(6) of the Holocaust understandable to me as specifically Jewish people. My attempt necessarily involved learning about Jewish religion, major trends of thought, customs, and values.

By 1980, the Holocaust had assumed major proportion within my thinking. In my Weltanschauung,(7) the Holocaust constituted <u>the most dis-orienting event in the twentieth century</u>. As a direct consequence of my outlook, I found that I could not morally justify direct association with any group or ideology which had been intimately involved in the Final Solution of the Jewish people. For me, to see Christian theology relatively intact after the Holocaust event was quite troublesome. It was, after all, anti-Judaic teaching and preaching derived from that same theology which contributed to the Nazi terror. I saw no way for contemporary Christianity (that is, post-Holocaust Christianity) to express its message without being at the same time anti-Judaic. In the course of the year-long preparation of my research paper on the Holocaust, I arrived at the point at which I no longer could reconcile being Christian with what had been perpetrated by Christians and through Christian teachings. On an intellectual and theological level, I came to see the Holocaust as a problem in theodicy with which Christianity was not at all prepared to grapple meaningfully. The traditional Christian affirmation about evil, (and at that time in my life, my affirmation also) that the world is fundamentally changed following the death and Resurrection of Christ, could not withstand the test of Auschwitz in my thinking. The historian Karl Löwith, introduced to me in the writing of Thomas A. Idinopulos,(8) proved to be a significant shaper of my concept and understanding of human history. Löwith wrote that history before and <u>after</u> Christ was, and is, not qualitatively different in terms of evil.(9) Löwith's book, <u>Meaning in History</u>, demonstrated to me for the first time that there are many interpretations of temporal history, with Christianity's version being one of the many schemes advanced. I imagine that I had always rather unquestioningly accepted the Christian interpretation of reality.

Allow me to draw together what I have tried to convey. My rejection of the Christian tradition as something of importance to me occurred at two levels: fundamental theological problems with basic Christian affirmations, and knowledge of Christian involvement, both directly and subtly, in the Holocaust of the Jewish people. The second level mentioned follows directly from my placement of great emphasis upon the

Holocaust. If that event were not significant in my mind, Christian involvement and silence would not have been so serious a matter to me. As to the first level, Bertrand Russell focused many of my theological problems with Christianity in his volume Why I Am Not a Christian.

Once my moorings with the Christian tradition had been disengaged, it was over a year before I felt ready to undergo conversion to Judaism. After all, not being aligned with Christianity does not necessarily place one in accord with Judaism. One can certainly respect the Jewish religion and the principles espoused therein without converting. When I rejected Christianity, I lost G-d and both a sense of, and respect for, any spiritual dimension. Much of the loss of a general spiritual overlay in my life can also be linked with my reaction to my mother's death in 1977. Her death at age forty-nine was another problem in theodicy for which Christianity had no meaningful response. One can, of course, easily field the theodicy problem by disallowing a spiritual dimension in life. If there is no G-d, then there cannot be any legitimate question of reconciling Him with evil in the world. Again, Bertrand Russell's volume was very much a part of my becoming alienated from any spiritual viewpoint.

It may well be at this point to trace my wife's and my contact with living Judaism and Jewish people. As early as 1976, we attended a Shabbat service at a Conservative synagogue in suburban Philadelphia. The service was primarily in Hebrew. Both the language and structure of the service proved to be quite mysterious to one used to church worship. In the Oneg Shabbat gathering after the service, we were both welcomed until it was learned we were not Jewish. From that juncture in the evening, we were viewed a bit suspiciously. Were we doing a research project on Judaism for college? Why did we come? people wanted to know. Our attendance was best explained in terms of our interest in and curiosity about Judaism.

Near the time of our college graduation in May of 1979, we had our first personal contact with a rabbi -- Rabbi Nason Goldstein. We met this particular rabbi at Lebanon Valley College during the course of a chapel convocation on the Holocaust. Because I was involved in the convocation proceedings, I had the opportunity to meet Rabbi Goldstein afterwards. Several days later, I called him to discuss the possibility of our becoming

Jewish. He urged us to discuss our thought of conversion with our Christian clergy before proceeding further. Incidentally, Rabbi Goldstein is a Conservative rabbi.

In July of 1979, we moved our family to York, Pennsylvania. In the weeks that followed our arrival, we contacted the one Conservative rabbi in the city. He vehemently discouraged our desire to convert, citing the specter of anti-Semitism. He argued that to be born Jewish is one thing, but to accept willingly the burden of being Jewish for reasons other than intermarriage is quite another. The overwhelming majority of people who convert to Judaism in America do so by virtue of the fact that they were marrying a Jew. We did not pursue our intentions with this particular rabbi after our first meeting. In fairness, it should be pointed out that there does exist a rabbinic injunction charging rabbis to actively discourage potential converts. We learned rather quickly that Judaism is not a proselytizing religion.

It was Rabbi Irwin Goldenberg, the Reform rabbi in York, who finally extended understanding and acceptance of our nebulous feeling about Judaism. Our learning process with Rabbi Goldenberg began in February of 1980 and continued for over a year. We attended temple worship services as often as we were able. Of special interest to me was that Rabbi Goldenberg was at that time, and remains, vitally interested in my Holocaust writing and research.

Let me return to my religious journey from Christianity through the gray area of non-spiritualism to Judaism. I believe that I moved in the direction of Judaism following the interim stages because of a profound need within myself to recognize a spiritual dimension in life. As a Christian, I had a close, personal relationship with G-d. Indeed, I experienced the nearness of G-d more than the closeness of other people many times. It was precisely because I missed the spiritual element that I could not espouse agnosticism or unitarianism in any long-term commitment. I chose Judaism as the expression of my spiritual needs because for me, it is the only system of values which possesses moral credibility after the Holocaust. I could not accept the value systems not only of the perpetrators of the Final Solution, but more significantly, those of the rest of the world which remained silent or confounded efforts to help the Jews. Though my choice appears to be the acceptance of the least evil, the least morally bankrupt system; it was nonetheless based upon a recognition of very positive aspects of the Jewish value system. The combination of spirituality, ritual, and an emphasis upon the human intellect serves in part to illustrate those positive elements. However, the most eloquent testimony to the value, strength, and viability of the Jewish tradition is offered by the affirmations of the Death Camp survivors of their faith and their Jewishness. Perhaps a significant factor in my decision to become a Jew was what the Jewish philosopher Emil L. Fackenheim(10) refers to as the 614th commandment. Rabbi Fackenheim has taken the liberty of adding one more mitzvah to the traditional listing of 613. He claims that to do no more than remain a Jew after the Holocaust is to confront the demons of Auschwitz in all their guises.(11) I wish to bear witness against the forces that made HaShoah a reality. I felt I could do this best as a Jew. It is noteworthy that in formulating this commandment, Dr. Fackenheim asserts that "we are forbidden,...to deny or despair of God, however much we may have to contend with him or belief in him...."(12) Therefore, despite its apparent reduction of Judaism to mere survivalism, the 614th commandment does call for a G-d centered faith!

Because my discovery of Judaism as a religious experience was strongly coupled with my contemplation and study of the greatest destruction in the history of the Jewish people, my perception of and feelings about Judaism are necessarily tinted with apprehension. I am very much concerned with being personally exposed to latent or overt anti-Judaicism. Because of fear, I am not yet able to do such a simple (yet meaningful) act as wearing a kippa(13) all of the time. As mentioned previously, I am concerned about the impact of my decision upon my daughter. The National Socialists had defined a Jew to be one who had practicing Jewish grandparents as far back as 1870. The choice of a person to be a Jew in 1870 adversely affected his grandchildren and great-grandchildren seventy years later in 1940. One must also recall that the Nazis did not differentiate between those people born as Jews and those who had converted to Judaism from without. Converting to Judaism from Christianity in particular is something which I have great difficulty telling other people. Being born Jewish is one thing; rejecting Christianity to espouse Judaism is indeed another -- almost as if one held the Truth in his hand, and let it go. I attribute the uneasiness which I have described to my having approached Judaism by way of observing the violently destructive forces brought to bear upon it in the Nazi era. My decision to convert also took into account the possibility that writing about the Holocaust as a Jew could have less impact upon a general readership than writing as a neutral, objective observer. It could, and has been argued, that Jews have an ax to grind concerning their experiences from 1933-45 in Europe. The path by which my wife came to Judaism was primarily through reading positive accounts thereof. Books detailing the religious and ethnic aspects of Jewish life written by such authors as Epstein, Donin, Wouk, and Fast were her vehicles to conversion.(14) As a result, my wife does not experience the same difficulty as I in saying she is Jewish or in practicing Judaism publicly in her daily life.

To summarize briefly, I have come to use the Holocaust as a measuring device to gauge the validity of ideologies, religious traditions, institutions, and thought patterns. I chose Judaism as my religious tradition because in Western culture, the Jewish tradition is the only system of life to have emerged after 1945 with any moral validity. I have also come to affirm the reality of G-d.

My affirmation of G-d brings me back again to the current stage of my odyssey within the Jewish tradition, namely, moving towards an halachic or Orthodox conversion. There are those people who may assert at this point that my conversion to Reform Judaism was perhaps understandable, but converting to the Orthodox tradition is really quite excessive. Valid response to my understanding of the Holocaust is one thing, but why go overboard to Orthodoxy?

My wife and I were drawn to consideration of Orthodox conversion shortly after our Reform conversion by reason of our plans to make <u>aliyah</u>(15) to Israel. Because of an internal misunderstanding within the Aliyah Office to which we applied, our Reform conversion was judged insufficient to make aliyah. We therefore began to learn about the requirements of Orthodox conversion. This was not only for our own sakes, but we wanted our daughter to be able to marry eventually in Israel. A Reform conversion would not be accepted as adequate for her to marry a Jew in Israel. In the four years since our Reform conversion, the legitimacy of that conversion vis-a-vis the Israeli Law of Return has been upheld. We now have the right to emigrate to Israel if we so desire. Despite the fact that we do not now need Orthodox conversion, we continue in that direction. As with our initial conversion to Judaism, my wife and I support each other's motives and progress towards Halachah. Though our pathways are not identical, with mine again profoundly connected with HaShoah, our objective remains the same.

We have come to see Reform Judaism as not really calling Jews to be a separate community in any real, tangible sense. It has been our observation that Reform Jews do not live life in a way fundamentally different from the remainder of society. Reform Judaism now appears to be a religion without much distinguishing contour, infused heavily with rationality and secularism. It should be said that one of the elements of the Reform tradition which initially attracted me was the emphasis upon the intellectual and the rational. This emphasis was, at the time of my first contact with Reform, a refreshing change from Christianity's frequent lack of openness to intellectually-based religious questioning. What has emerged from my reflection on the Holocaust is an understanding of the need for some sense of the Transcendent(16) in our rational, scientific world. It is precisely the notion of a transcendent reality, G-d if you will allow, that Reform Judaism does not strongly affirm. G-d is left to the individual conscience to accept or reject. One of the essential questions emerging from the Holocaust is: How are we to direct our intelligence in morally sound channels? In accordance with Arthur Schopenhauer(17) and Sören Kierkegaard,(18) I submit that morality is independent of reason, rationality, and intellect. Humanism, for example, premised upon the foundations of enlightened reason and rationality, does not provide any compelling reason not to commit murder. Belief in G-d, however, carries with it the obligation to behave in morally sound ways. It will be when man comes to realize that he needs the behavioral restraints of a spiritual dimension that mankind will begin to be secure from annihilation. Because I see that a reinvestment in spiritualness is called for in light of the Holocaust, I therefore feel drawn towards Orthodoxy. Despite contemporary intellectual bias to the contrary, several philosophers including Ludwig Wittgenstein and Paul K. Feyerabend have suggested that our selection of science (with its methodology founded upon reason and rationality) as the means of knowing about reality over and above the non-rational means (faith, for example) was an arbitrary act.(19) We in the twentieth century have come to assume that mythic expression(20) and human spirituality yield faulty perceptions when applied to the task of interpreting and understanding life in general. Yet science's claim to the Truth is valid only at selected points where reality impinges upon our senses in quantitative terms.(21) The limited scope of science is apparent when we consider that anything not detectable by our senses, either directly or with the aid of instruments, is essentially unknowable to science. Nonetheless, science, reason, and rationality are the functional gods of our time, with a resultant contempt for the Transcendent.(22) A scene from the motion picture The Chosen(23) is particularly appropriate here. Danny Saunders, the son of an Chasidic rebbe, tells his friend Reuven: My father is trapped by his own world (his Orthodoxy). The fact may well be, however, that we who treat all things in a rational manner are just as trapped ideologically. There are only certain pathways rationality can accept and flow in, just as with Orthodoxy. Orthodox Judaism fulfills a vital role as a counterbalance to modern rationalism. Premised upon faith from the beginning, Orthodox Judaism does not go out of its way to buttress its position with scientific and rational theories. Faith to the observant Jew is not to be found at the end of a long quest, by leaping over the stumbling blocks that reason cannot clear away. Rather, the way <u>begins</u> with faith. My search for Halachah, therefore, is based to some extent upon my recognition that it is a significant countervailing force to what I perceive as an alienating and destructive trend -- namely, the use of rationality and science as the <u>sole</u> means of knowing about anything.(24) I object to <u>extra scientiam nulla salus</u>,(25) and have tried to respond in a manner consistent with what I believe.

An extremely important dynamic in our movement toward Orthodox conversion is our relationship with an Orthodox individual in Los Angeles. This person read and responded to my wife's article in the <u>The Jewish Spectator</u> concerning our conversion to Reform Judaism. He has been a source of literally a new world of Orthodox literature and insight. He has provided much in the way of practical assistance in home observance of Halachah.

The final factor which I can identify as having bearing upon my pursuit of Orthodoxy again is linked to my study of the Holocaust. It is certainly a fact that many Jews who had assimilated into Western European culture were victims of the Nazi Endlösung.(26) Though many Jews had given up their Jewishness as a religious commitment and maintained merely ethnic bonds, they were, nonetheless, murdered along with the Orthodox Jews. Non-observance of the mitzvot does not relieve one of his Jewishness in the eyes of the world. The Nazis graphically demonstrated this point. As opposed to those Jews who had largely assimilated, Torah-observant Jews who were also victims of the Holocaust had something transcendent upon which to draw.(27) The latter's relationship with G-d would have provided some context, albeit inadequate perhaps, into which they could place their suffering. The Jews who did not strongly identify with Deity, it would seem to me, would have been so alone in the jaws of the Nazi onslaught. Reason provides little haven in the midst of unbearable pain. If I am going to be Jewish, I want to be so in a full sense that provides spiritual substance.

For the aforementioned reasons, I came to see the positive elements of Orthodox Judaism over and above Reform. After my separation from the Christian tradition, I experienced a spiritual vacuum in the shape of G-d(28) which I now believe frumkeit(29) can fill.

Discussing my conversion to Judaism in the course of lecturing to college students, I have encountered several related questions that deserve expanded consideration: Why did I abandon my Christian heritage? Might I not have stayed within the Christian tradition and struggled to effect those changes I felt to be necessary in the light of the Holocaust? Did I really give Christianity a chance since I encountered Judaism and the Holocaust? Why didn't I see Christianity as being reformable?

As I hope has been made apparent, my conversion to Judaism was not a whimsical decision. The discouragement received from those rabbis initially contacted served well to provoke reconsideration of our idea. For twenty-five years, Christianity had been an integral part of my life and my decision-making. The last ten years of those twenty-five were, of course, when I was most cognizant of my Christian value system. My conscious decision to reject Christianity was founded upon fundamental problems with basic Christian affirmations. Stated simply, I do not believe Jesus of Nazareth was the fulfillment of Jewish messianic hopes.(30) Therefore, the central Christian affirmation of accomplished redemption through Jesus' Crucifixion and Resurrection, is something I cannot accept. My staying within the Christian tradition for any length of time would not have altered the Church's basic tenets of faith. Insofar as specific changes in the Christian perspective to be made in light of HaShoah, sensitive religious education and offsetting commentary delivered during the liturgy may effect the needed attitudinal changes towards Jews and Judaism. However, such efforts will most likely take generations to blunt the cumulative effect of nineteen hundred years of theological anti-Judaism. Negative images of Jews long outlive the "usefulness"(31) they may once have had. I felt I could not sit on a "theological fence" and wait for evolutionary changes to occur. Given post-Holocaust Christianity's record and rate of change, I feel justified in the assumption of a multi-generational time scheme. I wanted to have a spiritual tradition in my own lifetime that I could affirm with a good conscience. At present, I am but in infancy with respect to knowledge and practice of Judaism. Building a personal Jewish tradition will take years, and that is the primary reason why I dissociated completely from my Christian background. If I was going to form a new relationship with a new tradition, I needed time in which to do so. I could not wait ten or fifteen years to further measure the metamorphosis of Christianity vis-a-vis Judaism. I have been asked by a middle-aged Jewish individual: If the Jewish people were to perpetrate a Holocaust on another group, would my conscience then dictate that I find another religious tradition and convert to it? In response, I do not consider myself so capricious as to change my total perspective towards life (which is what I believe religion to be) even twice. The psychological cost of such diametric change is too high to expend again. I am also not convinced that Jews, given their particular historical background and recent devastation in Europe, are going to commit organized murder on a scale beginning to approach the Nazi extermination program. Another question I have encountered related to conversion involved my daughter. How would I feel if she converted to Christianity as a young adult? Both my wife and I are working hard to provide our daughter Becky with a strong sense of Jewish roots. This process is made difficult because we live thirty-five miles from the nearest Jewish community. There are probably less than ten Jewish families in the county in which we reside. In addition, the prevailing religious and ethnic attitudes among the people in this county are anti-Catholic, anti-black, anti-Hispanic, and anti-Jewish. These attitudes are usually expressed subtly. I would have to strongly consider the possibility that if Becky were to convert to Christianity, her decision might be the result of cultural coercion rather than religious conviction. I would certainly feel a sense of disappointment and shortcoming in my efforts should she convert to Christianity. Perhaps she could, however, discover within the Christian tradition the meaning and sense of direction I could not find there.

>We have lived in numberless towns and villages; and in too many of them we have endured cruel suffering. Some we have forgotten; others are sealed into our memory, a wound that does not heal. A hundred generations of victims and martyrs; still their blood cried out from the earth. And so many, so many at Dachau, at Buchenwald, at Babi Yar, and...
>
>They lived with faith. Not all, but many. And surely, many died with faith; faith in God, in life, in the goodness that even flames cannot destroy. May we find a way to the strength of that faith, that trust, that sure sense that life and soul endure beyond this body's death.
>
>   <u>Gates</u> <u>of</u> <u>Prayer</u>

NOTES

CHAPTER III

THE HOLOCAUST AND MY CONVERSION TO JUDAISM

1. My background as a Christian was Lutheran, specifically Eastern Synod. I felt a very strong faith commitment to Christianity during my teen years and early twenties. Until I entered college, my knowledge of the Christian tradition and the Lutheran expression thereof was derived primarily from Sunday school classes, church worship services, and three years of catechetical classes.

My wife's religious background was Baptist and Roman Catholic. We were married in the Roman Catholic church. For further explanation of my wife's conversion process, see Nancy T. Frey, "My Road to Judaism," Jewish Spectator 47(1982): 50-52.

2. Halachic conversion:

The term Halachah in the Jewish tradition refers to "the road" or "the way of life". This term is associated with the Hebrew word derech which means "road" or "path". Halachah is often inaccurately translated as "law" in a narrow, legalistic sense.

Within the spectrum of Jewish tradition are the following branches: Orthodox, Conservative, Reconstructionist, and Reform. None of these branches of faith is a monolithic entity, but has within it subdivisions and distinct groups. In the Orthodox community, for example, are the Modern Orthodox (leftwing), the Agudath Israel International Organization (centrist), and the Chasidim (rightwing) along with other distinct groups. The Jewish Observer periodical, published in New York, is one voice of the mainline Orthodox community.

To elucidate the concept of an halachic conversion, let us present some of the salient requirements one must fulfill. An halachic conversion brings the convert into the Orthodox Jewish community. The requirements outlined below are those binding upon a male:

1) Study of Judaism under the auspices of an Orthodox rabbi.

2) An affirmation of the basic principles of the Jewish faith.

3) Sincere resolve to observe the <u>mitzvot</u>, "commandments", in everyday living. Included here would be daily Torah study, observing the dietary laws (<u>kashruth</u>), observing the Family Purity Laws, and daily prayer (<u>davening</u>).

4) Circumcision with the intent of conversion, or if previously circumcised, the rite of <u>hatafat dam brit</u>, "a letting of a spot of blood".

5) Immersion in a <u>kosher</u>, "ritually correct", <u>mikvah</u>, "ritual bath".

6) Acceptance of a Hebrew name given by the <u>Beth din</u>, "the rabbinic court". The three rabbis comprising the court must be members in good standing in religious (Orthodox) Jewry. Orthodox Jews are also known as Torah-observant Jews, observant Jews, Torah Jews, and religious Jews.

The Orthodox branch of Judaism does not recognize conversions performed by a rabbi from any other branch of Judaism as legitimate. Therefore, having undergone Reform conversion, I am still considered a gentile by the Orthodox community. However, I am viewed as a Jew by the Reform tradition <u>as well as by non-Jews</u>. In addition, the <u>Law of Return</u> enacted by the government of the State of Israel makes no distinction as to which branch conducted the conversion. Once converted to Judaism in the Reform tradition, a person may go to Israel and immediately become an Israeli citizen with the accompanying responsibilities and privileges. In effect, the Law of Return does not restrict immigration to and citizenship in Israel to only those individuals born of a Jewish mother (the traditional definition of a Jew). All Jews are officially welcome in the State of Israel. For more on conversion as it affects one's status in Israel, see Barbara Sofer, "Who Is a Convert?," <u>Israel Scene</u> 3(1982): 13-18.

In contradistinction to Orthodox or halachic conversion, a Reform conversion involves a period of learning about Judaism from a rabbi, the taking of a Hebrew name, reciting the first line of the faith affirmation Shema (Shema Yisroel, Adonai Elohenu, Adonai Echad -- "Hear, O Israel: the L-rd is our G-d, the L-rd is One"), and having the ceremony conducted in the presence of two witnesses. Conservative conversion involves the outward manifestations of an halachic conversion. However, such manifestations are performed as ritual rather than as mitzvot, and the legitimacy of the officiating Conservative rabbis is questionable from an halachic standpoint. The legitimacy is suspect because the rabbis, being Conservative, deny basic tenets of Judaism -- especially the divinity of the Torah. See also Nisson Wolpin, "The Case of the Non-Conserving Conservatives," Jewish Observer 16(1983): 4-9.

3. As a student in college, I elected to take many more religion courses than were required by general academic curriculum standards. The college I attended, Lebanon Valley College in Annville, Pennsylvania, is a small Methodist-supported school with the religion courses definitely reflecting a pro-Christian perspective. At the same time, however, the approach taken within the specific religion courses was definitely academic as opposed to apologetic or polemical. Despite the overlay of Christian perspective, a serious attempt was made to examine such topics as various religious traditions, the bible, church history, Jesus' life and ministry, and Near East archeology with objectivity and scholarly candor. It was in these courses that Judaism was discussed in detail simply because of the theological and historical nexus of Christianity with Judaism.

4. My research paper, "Issues in Post-Holocaust Christian Theology", appeared in the Summer, 1983 issue of Dialog. Dialog, a scholarly periodical published in Minnesota, is associated with the Lutheran church.

5. See A. Roy Eckardt, "Christians and Jews: Along a Theological Frontier," Encounter 40(1979): 97, for the citation of Haim Cohn's work.

6. Prototypic victims refers to the Jews.

7. The German word Weltanschauung is translated as "philosophy of life, outlook, worldview, and ideology". Die Welt contributes "world" to the meaning; die Anschauung contributes "conception, mode of viewing, and idea". Liberally translated, the word becomes "overarching meaning of life".

8. See Thomas A. Idinopulos, "Christianity and the Holocaust," *Cross Currents* 28(1978): 260.

9. See Karl Löwith, *Meaning in History*, pp. 190-91.

10. Emil Ludwig Fackenheim (1916-) is a Canadian rabbi and theologian considered to be a religious existentialist. He was born in Halle, Germany and is currently professor of philosophy at the University of Toronto.

11. See Emil L. Fackenheim, *The Jewish Return into History*, pp. 19-24 for an expansion of his proposed 614th commandment. The commandment reads: "...*the authentic Jew of today is forbidden to hand Hitler yet another, posthumous victory.*" *Ibid.*, p. 22. Rabbi Fackenheim insists that his use of the *mitzvah* motif has no anti-Orthodox implications.

12. *Ibid.*, p. 24.

13. A *kippa* or *yarmulke* is a head covering worn by observant Jewish males.

14. The specific books that my wife read concerning Judaism include:

Isidore Epstein, *Judaism*; Hayim Halevy Donin, *To Be A Jew*; Hayim Halevy Donin, *To Raise a Jewish Child*; Herman Wouk, *This Is My God*; and Howard Fast, *The Jews*.

15. *Aliyah* means "to ascend"; in the case of going to Israel, the term means "to immigrate".

16. The term *Transcendent* is used here in the sense of a spiritual reality beyond human empirical verification. The notion of transcendence "--is beyond proof or disproof: it is not an object of knowledge. But the idea of it is. Therefore, the intrinsic merits of its meaning become the sole measure of its credibility, and the appeal of such meaning remains as the sole ground of possible belief--...." Hans Jonas, "Immortality and the Modern Temper," *Harvard Theological Review* 55(1962): 1. Jonas seems to be saying that if the notion of a transcendent reality speaks to the human condition in a meaningful way, then it has the chance of becoming accepted and believed.

17. Arthur Schopenhauer (1788-1860) was a German philosopher.

18. Soren Kierkegaard (1813-1855) was a Danish philosopher and theologian.

19. Ludwig Wittgenstein's assertion concerning science was drawn from the work of George M. Kren and Leon Rappoport, The Holocaust and the Crisis of Human Behavior, p. 139. Wittgenstein, a twentieth-century philosopher, is best known for his thoughts on language and its implications. Paul K. Feyerabend is a contemporary philosopher whose work draws heavily upon that of John Stuart Mill.

George M. Kren is a professor in the Department of History at Kansas State University in Manhattan, Kansas. Leon Rappoport is a professor in the Department of Psychology at the same university.

20. Mythic expression, according to Paul K. Feyerabend, is a sociological rather than a mathematical explanation of reality.

21. See Aryeh Carmell and Cyril Domb. eds., Challenge, p. 51.

The apparent paradoxes inherent in religious traditions and affirmations are usually pointed out by detractors and cynics. An example of such a paradox is the existence of evil in the world while at the same time there is an all-powerful, beneficent G-d supposedly in control of human history. Yet it must also be made apparent that science lives with its own paradoxes. Light, for example, is accepted simultaneously as both a wave and a particle. This note was borrowed from Carmell and Domb.

22. Richard L. Rubenstein seems to place the blame for our contemporary application of rational, scientific mentality to all aspects of life squarely upon the shoulders of Torah Judaism. It is Rubenstein's contention that "for the believer God alone is sacred. Since no spirits exist to be appeased, rationality can replace magic as the fundamental mode of problem-solving in all areas of human activity." Richard L. Rubenstein, The Age of Triage, p.2. Rubenstein faults biblical monotheism for modern modes of problem-solving because, in his estimation, monotheism allowed for the accounting of all physical phenomena by a unified set of principles. G-d was relegated to a

sphere beyond this world. Temporal processes were thus removed from supernatural explanation.

The Roman Catholic theologian and social ethicist John T. Pawlikowski echoed my concern about the need for transcendent values when he interpreted the three primary causes of the Holocaust to be bureaucracy, technology, and the erosion of transcendental values. Pawlikowski's idea here was part of a lecture he delivered on 7 March 1983 at the Bernhard E. Olson Scholar's Conference on the Holocaust in New York.

23. The film The Chosen was adapted from Chaim Potok, The Chosen, a novel.

24. Richard L. Rubenstein sees contemporary religious professionals (the clergy) as being trained and imbued with the rational-scientific spirit of our era. He doubts that any transformation of contemporary life can emerge from organized religion as long as its spokespeople reflect the modern spirit. Rubenstein cites the modern seminary and college academic tool of textual criticism to illustrate his point about training. Rubenstein, Age of Triage, p. 234. The premise of textual criticism is that the bible is but another good piece of literature or another historical document to be dissected.

25. Extra scientiam nulla salus, "no knowledge outside science", was borrowed from Paul K. Feyerabend, Against Method.

26. Endlösung is the German term for the Final Solution.

27. It should be pointed out, however, that many Torah-observant Jews rejected their faith in the face of their terrible suffering. This is in no way judgment of their action. Some scholars have interpreted rejection of faith in response to HaShoah as the only meaningful faith statement, notwithstanding the apparent paradox.

28. The spiritual vacuum metaphor was shared with me by Ms. Naomi Abramowitz.

29. Frumkeit is a Yiddish term meaning "Torah-observant living; Orthodox Jewish practice".

30. It is my opinion that Jesus was most probably aligned with the Zealots in first-century Palestine. My opinion is based upon Jesus' anti-Roman and pro-Jewish stance, and his desire to establish the Jewish kingdom on earth. I do not believe that Jesus was G-d or the Son of G-d; rather he was an observant Jew.

31. "Usefulness" of negative images of Jews and Judaism may be understandable to a degree if we consider the ecclesiastical struggle of mainline Judaism with the fledgling Christian sect in the first century of the common era.

CHAPTER IV

SOME JEWISH PERSPECTIVES ON HaSHOAH

There are four major divisions within Judaism. It is first necessary to understand what Judaism is before the various groups can be defined. Because Western civilization has learned about religious traditions in general from Christianity, it sees most everything as being able to be easily categorized. With respect to Judaism, this categorization breaks down. In the Christian Weltanschauung Judaism is seen as a religion. It is, however, much more than that. Jews are a people, not a race as is often mistakenly supposed. The difference lies in the fact that a race consists of a group of people with the same genetic heritage. Jews, as a people, do not all share the same genetic background.(1) Ethnicity is also part of being Jewish, but that is not monolithic either. There are different ethnic groups within Judaism, the most notable being Sephardic(2) and Askenazic(3) Jews. Judaism is perceived by Western civilization as another religion. Again, this is a false assumption. It is an entire way of life, not just a religion. There is no dogma or specific set of faith statements which one must accept in order to be a Jew. A person is born a Jew. Unlike Christianity, wherein being born of Christian parents does not necessarily make one a Christian, one is a Jew at birth regardless of his religious orientation.(4) A child born to Christian parents is not a Christian until and unless he is baptized and accepts the necessary faith statements with respect to Jesus. Those statements vary across Christian denominational lines, but they are necessary to being Christian.

One can become a Jew by conversion.(5) The act of choosing Judaism is generally held to be a religious experience. There is no contradiction with the above statements however, because while not solely a religion, Judaism does encompass that aspect of life also. The distinctions among the four major groups within Judaism can best be made apparent on theological grounds, although the differences encompass much more.

The first branch of Judaism for discussion is Orthodoxy, also known as traditional Judaism. It must be noted here that there are subdivisions within each group, most especially Orthodoxy.(6) In the Orthodox tradition one conforms to definite behavioral guidelines which affect every aspect of daily life and one

lines which affect every aspect of daily life and one subscribes to specific faith statements. These guidelines are the mitzvot,(7) "commandments of G-d to His chosen people". Examples of specific mitzvot are kashruth, "dietary laws"; Family Purity pertaining to sexual conduct especially within marriage; shabbos(8) "the sabbath day"; and davening, "prayer". The daily practices of Orthodox Jews are almost identical with those of Jews centuries ago. Within Orthodoxy, change occurs slowly and this pace is felt to be best.

Reform Judaism grew out of the nineteenth century German Jewish community's response to the Enlightenment.(9) It was a reaction against what was seen as the narrow, ghetto-mentality of the Orthodox. Change was swift and devastating. Many practices such as kashruth and Family Purity were seen as obsolete and discarded. Others, such as shabbos observance, were changed radically. At one point some reformers even changed shabbos from Saturday to Sunday.

Reaction to the sweeping changes of Reform from within the movement itself brought about the Conservative branch of Judaism. These people believed change to be necessary in some areas of Jewish life, but not at the sacrifice of Jewish identity. Their changes were less rapid and less radical. While Orthodoxy and Reform each knew where they stood and what they wanted, Conservative Jews found themselves more equivocating on many issues.

The Reconstructionist movement, founded in 1922 by Dr. Mordechai M. Kaplan,(10) is an attempt to redefine Judaism. It sees Judaism as "religious culturalism".(11) Reconstructionists perceive the religious foundations of Judaism as mythological structure devoid of reality.

This background information was included to provide the reader with an appreciation of the spectrum of Jewish belief, thereby allowing him to better understand Jewish response to the Holocaust. Each of the four groups discussed deals with the Holocaust according to its own value system. Treatment of the response within each group will necessarily be a generalization. The Final Solution is not easily dismissed by any Jew. If nothing more, HaShoah forces each and every Jew to realize the fragility of his existence in the world.

The Orthodox branch of Judaism has exhibited the least response to the Holocaust. For mainline and right-wing Orthodox, HaShoah is seen to be only the most recent example of Jewish suffering at the hands of the gentiles. The only meaning which they can attribute to the Holocaust is that it was the will of G-d, which man cannot fathom. The Orthodox would pronounce as blasphemous any view which holds that Israel was reparation and redemption for HaShoah.

Much of Orthodox Judaism was against the establishment of the State of Israel. They believed that the Jews would return to their Promised Land only with the coming of the Messiah. The Moshiach (Messiah) would be a human being who would sit on the throne of his ancestor, David. He would deliver the Jews from their suffering and usher in the messianic age. The Messiah is not a spiritual concept, but an historical reality. He would restore the Biblical land of Israel to the Jews, reign over the world in peace, and put an end to suffering.

Throughout the centuries Jews have believed that their suffering will hasten the arrival of the Messiah. Various false messiahs have arisen through the ages during or following eras of great suffering. Perhaps it is a tribute to the uniqueness of the Holocaust that no messianic hopefuls arose in its wake.

After the Chmielnicki massacres(12) in seventeenth century Poland the Jews were physically crushed. In 1648 Bogdan Chmielnicki lead the cossacks against their oppressors, the Polish noblemen. The Jews were in the middle of the conflict by reason of their occupations as collectors of taxes and administrators of the Polish economy. The killings occurred from approximately 1648 to 1658. In 1648 as the massacres were beginning in Poland a man named Sabbatai Zevi(13) proclaimed the advent of the messianic age. In 1665 Sabbatai Zevi announced himself as the Messiah, the anointed of G-d.(14) Jews perceived a connection between their suffering on Poland and the advent of the Messiah.

Other major Jewish catastrophes evoked similar, if less well known, messianic hopefuls. The Holocaust, however, was an event filled with such horror that no spiritual equivalent can be found. Therefore the extreme uniqueness of HaShoah, even in comparison with other major Jewish tragedies of the last two thousand years, is demonstrated by its lack of spiritual revitalization. Instead, many Jews turned away from spiri-

years, is demonstrated by its lack of spiritual revitalization. Instead, many Jews turned away from spiritual expectations to the idea of making Jewish survival depend on the Jews themselves and not on G-d.

Orthodox Jews believe that G-d directs the course of human history and no mere human being can understand His intent. The Jewish holiday of Purim can be used to illustrate this point. The Biblical book of Esther tells the story of how Haman, an evil advisor to the Babylonian king, plots to destroy the Jews living in exile. Due in part to Esther's intervention Haman and his heirs were killed instead. The celebration of this Jewish victory is called the festival of Purim.(15) The exact happenings are to be understood as G-d's way of covertly guiding the course of history. Likewise, Orthodoxy sees the Holocaust as another of G-d's workings. They cannot fathom the reason or meaning, but can only attribute it to the will of G-d which they do not presume to understand. The questions raised by non-Orthodox Jews with respect to this event are answered by the statement, "For the believer there aren't any questions and for the non-believer there are ultimately no answers."(16) This means that for the Orthodox Jew there are no questions which need to be asked; for the non-Orthodox Jew and the gentiles there are no answers to be found.

Reform Judaism, while not claiming to understand the Holocaust, responds to it by marking its remembrance in the liturgical calender. They observe Yom HaShoah(17) along with their observance of Yom HaAtzmaut(18). This is to blunt the negative weight of the Holocaust while linking these two events in people's minds.

The majority of Jewish "theological"(19) response to HaShoah has been expressed by persons who could not easily be categorized as belonging to one of the four major branches of Judaism. Many of these persons are theologians and/or philosophers. While not reflecting the view of a specific branch of Judaism, their perspectives on the Holocaust are of importance.

One Israeli scholar, Immanuel Hartom, sees HaShoah as divine retribution for the sin of assimilation.(20) Hartom's thought asserts that G-d directed the Holocaust to punish the Jews who were committing the sin of assimilating out of the world of Judaism and into the world of the gentiles. This contention is erroneous because the majority of those Jews exterminated were not assimilationist Jews. They were Eastern European Jews who kept the covenant. If G-d wanted to punish assimilation in the Jewish community, the Holocaust should have occurred in America! Furthermore, the logical result of HaShoah would be for more Jews to assimilate to prevent a similar fate for themselves and their families. Those Jews who could help reinvigorate the post-1945 Jewish community in observing the commandments were exactly those who were murdered.

Rabbi Joel Teitelbaum(21) offers a somewhat similar explanation of HaShoah. His allegation is that HaShoah is retribution for the sins of the Zionists. Yet again, Eastern European Jewry was largely non-Zionist. In addition, those Jews with an overwhelming urge to settle in the Biblical land of Palestine would have been the ones to have made greater attempts to escape Nazi Europe, defy the British blockade of Palestine, and settle in what they felt to be their homeland.

In both of the above cases it was the "wrong" Jews who were punished. The British Reform rabbi, Ignaz Maybaum,(22) solves that problem. He claims that those particular Jews who died did so as vicarious sufferers for the sins of others. This is almost equivalent to stating that since the vicarious suffering and death of one Jew in the first century had no appparent effect, G-d decided to try again with six million Jews in the twentieth century of the common era. It seems excessively cruel for G-d to cause those who explicitly followed His covenant to suffer and die in order to have those who did not begin observance anew. Such a G-d could not be called a G-d of love or mercy.

The viewpoint of the Jewish victims is one area of inquiry which has not been explored. Those who died may not have seen their deaths as a tragedy. For the observant Jews, it is preferable to die rather than transgress some of the mitzvot. The victims, upon realizing imminent death, would possibly have been glad to die as observant Jews to the sanctification of G-d's name. Granted they died, but they died as Jews. Certainly some Jews preyed upon Jews to attempt to prevent or delay their own deaths. Many of the victims would have preferred to die themselves rather than "stand by their brother's blood"(23) thereby transgressing the commandment wherein "<u>EVERY JEW IS RESPONSIBLE FOR EVERY OTHER JEW. ALWAYS.</u>"(24) Also, S.S. Sturmbannführer

Adolf Eichmann(25) knew the Shema prayer,(26) indicating that many Jews recited it before they were executed (as would be true of observant Jews).(27)

The majority of the Jewish theologians concentrate their efforts upon justifying the possibility of faith after the Holocaust. "Rather than seeking solutions, they are engaged in articulating responses."(28) Some of those theologians include Eliezer Berkovits, Emil L. Fackenheim, Irving Greenberg, and Abraham Joshua Heschel. While response to the Holocaust is important, one cannot give up the attempt of attacking the problem of theodicy directly. Without an understanding of G-d's role in Auschwitz, one is forever plagued with uncertainty as to the nature of G-d given the fact of unfathomable evil. One cannot properly respond to an event which one cannot begin to comprehend or explain. Response without an attempt at understanding is futile.

Eliezer Berkovits sees a paradox with respect to G-d's presence in the world. It is necessary that G-d be present in the world in order to give meaning to life. At the same time, for human freedom to exist, G-d must be absent. For Berkovits, the only way to resolve this paradox is to postulate a hidden G-d who hides Himself at the same time that He reveals Himself to man.(29)

Another interpretation which reveals an attribute of G-d is provided by Abraham Joshua Heschel. He postulates divine pathos, that G-d suffers with his people. Therefore, when human suffering such as the Holocaust occurs, G-d also suffers along with the victims. Perhaps that is the price G-d must pay for having given free will to man.

Despite being an Orthodox rabbi, Irving Greenberg differs from much of the Orthodox sentiment with respect to the Holocaust. In his estimation HaShoah demands some "basic reorientation in light of it by the surviving Jewish community."(30) Greenberg contends that because approximately eighty percent of the observant Jewish intellectual base as of 1939 was exterminated by 1945, the survival of the Jewish community within the covenant of G-d has been radically endangered. Such a momentous event must serve as a source of reorientation for the entire Jewish community. Faith must be maintained and strengthened but HaShoah must be given consideration in any theological statement.

Professor Yaffa Eliach, in speaking of the Final Solution feels that, "it serves as an instant Judaizer by shocking people into Jewishness. ...It may instill a distorted view of Jewish self-image, Jewish gentile relations and the Jewish place in world history. The Holocaust presents the Jew as the ultimate victim...."(35) HaShoah is being used as a unifying force within the Jewish community. Courses, lectures, and discussions on the Holocaust, while important when properly utilized, are being misused as a way of drawing young people into becoming interested in their Jewish heritage. However, "the bonds which unify Jews must emanate not from a common tragedy but from the experience of a rich past, of which the Holocaust is only one aspect."(36) The positive elements of Jewishness should be the basis of rekindling interest in Judaism. Young Jews should be drawn toward their heritage by demonstration of a positive meaning in being a Jew, such as exists in the teshuva movement.(37) HaShoah has, or should have, much importance for Judaism in the areas of theological statements, historical background, and education. It most definitely should be fitted into the Jewish calendar. The last historical event integrated into that calendar was the Maccabean Revolt (165-142 B.C.E.), celebrated today as Chanukkah. The Holocaust should not, however, be used as the sole means of creating a Jewish identity in Jews with little or no emphasis upon personal involvement with Judaism.

Currently, the "martyrdom" of the six million is included in the religious observance of Tisha be-Av, which recalls the tragedies from the Jewish past. HaShoah should not be included under the same general observance as the destruction of the first Temple in 586 B.C.E. by the Babylonians, the second Temple's destruction in 70 C.E. by the Romans, and the War of Independence of the State of Israel in 1948. It should merit separate observance. As mentioned above, Reform Judaism observes Yom HaShoah in April of each year. In the Reform prayerbook are two meditations dealing with the Holocaust.(38) This type of observance of Auschwitz should be emulated by the rest of Judaism.

The thought of Richard L. Rubenstein, who is the most controversial Jewish theologian dealing with the Holocaust, has evolved over the years of his work thereupon. His earlier writing dealt with the idea of rejecting the G-d of history in favor of a return to a pagan-like god of Nature.(39) In a sense that idea cannot be seen as Jewish response since it requires the

Auschwitz is to be seen as revelation (31) according to Emil L. Fackenheim. Following HaShoah one can no longer cling to the hope of Sinai nor can one surrender to the despair of Auschwitz. Rather it is necessary to maintain a dialectic, or healthy tension, between hope and despair.(32) One of Fackenheim's theses is that G-d's voice could be heard at Auschwitz commanding His people to remain Jews in the face of their own annihilation. According to Fackenheim there are now 614 commandments. The additional one urges Jewish steadfastness lest Hitler achieve a posthumous victory in his war against the Jews.

As mentioned previously, the State of Israel is seen by some Jews to be reparation for the Holocaust. If this is so, the price was too high. Six million Jewish deaths in the defense of Israel would have been tragic, yet more acceptable. However, to postulate that they died so Israel could be born borders on the obscene. A <u>large percentage of those who died would have considered the establishment of a Jewish homeland without the prior advent of the Messiah to be a desecration of G-d's name</u>. Therefore, to say that their deaths occurred so that such a desecration would come to pass, is the height of insensitivity. In making statements with regard to HaShoah one must achieve a certain empathy with the orientation of the victims so as not to be offensive to their memories.

Among Jews, the Holocaust has been used for many purposes. Henry Friedlander cautions that, "...the Holocaust cannot be used to validate political positions."(33) This caveat is necessary for those who would use Auschwitz as a weapon for assuring support for the political State of Israel in the world community. Implicit in their arguments is the idea that after what was done to the Jews from 1933-45 the world owes it to those Jews still living to support Israel. Since Israel's continued existence is the only guarantee Jews have for their ultimate survival, a world which permitted the Nazi horror must now atone for its guilt by backing the State of Israel no matter what. Many Jews see the above statements as an absolute truth and therefore use HaShoah as a magic weapon when any action by the State of Israel is criticized by the world community.

Another caveat for the Jewish community is against the use of Auschwitz as "a surrogate for Jewish education, communal responsibility ... and creativity."(34)

acknowledgement of the termination of the covenant, thus ending the raison d'etre of Judaism. In his present volume, Rubenstein rejects the idea of a secular solution to modern problems. "...<u>A purely secular, rationalistic approach to our social problems is unlikely to produce the collective altruism our situation demands</u>. Without religious values, the preferred solution to a social problem is likely to be the one involving fewest costs."(40) He sees the need for a religious perspective to invest modern life with the values necessary to turn back from our <u>individualistic</u> cares, and begin genuinely caring about other human beings. Such religious transformation, "must be an inclusive vision appropriate to a global civilization in which Moses and Mohammed, Christ, Buddha, and Confucius all play a role. We can no longer rest content with a humanity divided into the working and the workless, the saved and the damned, the Occident and the Orient. Our fates are too deeply intertwined. The call for religious transformation is in reality a call to conversion, a call to change ourselves."(41)

Unfortunately, Rubenstein's "inclusive vision" seems to advocate a "United Nations of Religions". It is given no real explanation in terms of putting such an idea into a practical, workable form. This author sees an <u>enriching of the particular</u> to be a better solution. A sense of the Transcendent is necessary for contemporary problems to be solved in a moral manner. Each particular religious tradition needs to be strengthened in order to reinvest religious values with meaning for today. In the face of easily discarded humanistic values a firmer base for morality must be made apparent. Therefore the G-d of history must be revitalized for mankind to effect its social salvation.

NOTES

CHAPTER IV

SOME JEWISH PERSPECTIVES ON HaSHOAH

1. Due in large part to conversions, there are Jews of almost every race and from every country in the world. Physical characteristics range from nordic blonde to the richest black. Despite the caricatures of Jews it is not possible to determine who is Jewish merely by looking at people.

2. Sephardic Jews, sometimes referred to as Oriental Jews, consist of those who were from what is now Spain and the Mediterranean countries, including present-day Israel. In general, they speak Ladino, a form of Spanish dating from before the Inquisition.

3. Askenazic Jews are those from the Eastern European areas including Germany. They speak Yiddish among themselves. Yiddish is a form of Middle German which is written in Hebrew letters.

4. Being born of a Jewish mother is what makes one a Jew. If only one's father is Jewish, one is not Jewish.

5. See note number 2 for Chapter III, "The Holocaust and My Conversion to Judaism".

6. Mayer Schiller, "Welcome Back!," in The Road Back, pp. 221-44.

7. See Eliyahu Kitov, The Jew and His Home.

8. See Isidor Grunfeld, The Sabbath.

9. In Germany, the Enlightenment was known as die Aufklärung.

10. Meir Kahane, Why Be Jewish?, p. 46.

11. Ibid., p. 47.

12. Max L. Margolis and Alexander Marx, "The Chmielnicki Massacres," in A History of the Jewish People, pp. 551-57.

13. Margolis and Marx, "Sabbatai Zevi," in <u>History of the Jewish People</u>, pp. 558-67.

14. The <u>Moshiach</u>, "Messiah", in Jewish tradition is to be the anointed of G-d in the same way as King David was anointed when he assumed the throne. Moshiach is thought of in terms of an historical person, not a spiritual being.

15. See Nosson Scherman and Meir Zlotowitz, eds., <u>The Megillah/The Book of Esther</u>.

16. Robert Younger to Nancy T. Frey, 13 December 1982.

17. <u>Yom HaShoah</u>, "Day of the Destruction", is the annual Holocaust Remembrance service.

18. Yom HaAtzmaut is the celebration of the establishment of the State of Israel, which in the Jewish calendar falls on the fifth of Iyar.

19. Judaism does not have theology per se.

20. Byron L. Sherwin and Susan G. Ament, eds., <u>Encountering the Holocaust</u>, p. 409. Byron L. Sherwin is professor of Jewish Religious Thought at Spertus College of Judaica in Chicago.

21. <u>Ibid</u>.

22. <u>Ibid</u>.

23. Kahane, <u>Why Be Jewish?</u>, p. 200.

24. Robert Younger to Nancy T. Frey, 7 January 1983.

25. Adolf Eichmann, a member of the S.S. hierarchy, was present at the execution of Jews. That he knew the Shema prayer was brought out in interviews with Jews presented on the CBS television program "60 Minutes".

26. The Shema is the central Jewish affirmation of faith. <u>Shema Yisroel Adonai Elohainu Adonai Echad</u>, "Hear, O Israel: the L-rd is our G-d, the L-rd is One".

27. Michael Asheri, <u>Living Jewish</u>, pp. 104-05.

28. Sherwin and Ament, eds., Encountering the Holocaust, p. 414.

29. Ibid., p. 417.

30. Irving Greenberg, "Judaism and Christianity after the Holocaust," Journal of Ecumenical Studies 12(1975): 523.

31. Compare Michael B. Buser, Auschwitz as Revelation.

32. Sherwin and Ament, eds., Encountering the Holocaust, pp. 419-23.

33. Henry Friedlander, "Toward a Methodology of Teaching about the Holocaust," Teachers College Record 80(1979): 522.

34. Yaffa Eliach, "The Holocaust as Obligation and Excuse," Center for Holocaust Studies Newsletter 2(1980): 5. Professor Eliach is director of the Center for Holocaust Studies in New York.

35. Ibid.

36. Ibid., p. 9.

37. The teshuva movement is a recent occurrence within Orthodox Judaism whereby Jews who had no previous Jewish education are taught about being Jewish.

38. Chaim Stern, ed., Gates of Prayer, pp. 575, 628.

39. Richard L. Rubenstein, After Auschwitz.

40. Richard L. Rubenstein, The Age of Triage, p. 232.

41. Ibid., p. 240.

CHAPTER V

THE HOLOCAUST, SCIENTIFIC RATIONALITY,
AND TRANSCENDENCE: CRITIQUE AND SYNTHESIS

The task which I have set before myself is to attempt to make the Holocaust understandable as an event that occurred only forty years ago. This effort will not only involve explanation of the Holocaust event, but will also comprise the search for meaning. The Holocaust requires placement in some type of context for it to be comprehended at all. At the same time, the presence of this event within a given context needs further interpretation. If the Holocaust is an integral part of the twentieth century culture, which is one possible context, it must then be asked: How is the world to be seen differently? The scholars George M. Kren and Leon Rappoport aptly point out that "existing interpretations of the Holocaust -- or explanations masquerading as interpretations -- do not provide an adequate social, emotional, or historical 'ground' on which ordinary people may come to grips with it as a human event defining our culture..."(1) The assumption underlying Kren's and Rappoport's contention is that the Holocaust is public event and not to be seen exclusively within the confines of a Jewish context. There is certainly no denying that the Final Solution is part of the general history of twentieth century Western civilization. Our objectives, therefore, must be to place the Holocaust within the continuum of this century's events in an understandable manner, and then to draw overarching meaning as a result of that particular placement. Overarching meaning follows from such questions as: How is reality fundamentally changed after Auschwitz? and What worldview is morally defensible in the wake of the Endlösung? Consider the statement: The Holocaust, the complex and rational program of dehumanization and murder, occurred at the cultural and scientific fulcrum of Europe from 1933 to 1945. This declarative does not fit our mental construct of modern culture. The time period for the Holocaust would be much more credible in the statement: The Final Solution occurred in central Europe shortly after the fall of the Roman Empire. Yet not only is the time frame of the Endlösung problematic for our modern consciousness, but considering the event to be rational renders it almost unassimilable. It may be well to examine several of the explanations and interpretations already advanced regarding the Holocaust, pointing out in each what this author perceives as shortcomings.

In apparent attempts to overcome cognitive dissonance(2) about the rational, contemporary nature of the Ausrottung(3) of the European Jews, many scholars, theologians, and laypersons conceive of the Holocaust as a gross aberration, a bizarre throwback into uncivilized times. Auschwitz and Treblinka are seen in terms of an irrational, anti-Semitic outburst, a dark chapter in history, or a demonic evil. Certainly extermination of the Jewish people in Europe was not the action of a Western, Christian nation whose people were educated in the rational spirit of the modern world. The assumption underpinning the aberration notion is that the Western world is moving essentially in a sane, morally progressive path. Thus, the explanations offered for l'holocauste are in terms of demonstrating just how far outside the mainstream of Western history this event really lies. Proponents of this approach to "solving" the Holocaust ask such questions as, How could this Awe-ful Event have occurred? According to this rational, scientific mode of inquiry, the Holocaust is viewed as a "problem to be solved".(5) The pathway that this approach takes vis-a-vis the Holocaust is to explain in great detail "'what led to what'" in "sociohistorical sequence".(6) The common story thread of explanation might be condensed as follows. A widespread decay in German morality caused by socio-economic stress(7) permitted a psychopath and his henchmen to trample freely over law, conscience, and innate goodness. The thinking evidenced in this summary is that something had to have gone wrong with society for the Death Camps to have been in operation -- a breakdown in morality, economy, law or rationality. Implicit in the aberration perspective is the idea that if all the institutionally-supported values had been intact in 1933, a Holocaust would never have occurred. Yet is it not precisely in those times of social and political stress that our institutions and values are to function to maintain behavior in civilized channels? What emerges from the story presented above are conceptions of the Holocaust in terms of individual and group psychopathology, uncritical obedience to authority,(8) and anti-Semitism. The horror, depravity, hatred, and insanity of HaShoah are accentuated therein. "This general approach presents the Holocaust as a kind of morality play justifying the ideals of Western liberal democracy by showing what can happen when madmen gain power and racism is allowed to prevail."(9) Therefore, not only can the problem of Nazism and the Final Solution be explained via this methodology, but liberal, enlightened democracy is made the benefactor of the explanation. The net result of perceiving the

Holocaust as an atypical historical event is to explain it in terms we can cope with and comprehend. Though the event was admittedly more technically sophisticated in the means of killing devised; it remains, according to this line of thinking, explicable in terms with which we are familiar. Included among the lessons this approach derives from HaShoah are: anti-Semitism must be prevented, we must remember(10) the Holocaust so that it will not be repeated, traditional religion must be bolstered to provide needed moral guidelines, and constitutional democracy must be maintained as a countervailing force to totalitarianism.(11) Phrased simply, to prevent another Holocaust, we need only strengthen Western values, governments, and economies.

A corollary to this first Holocaust theory places HaShoah within the context of other genocides and tragedies. When in this context, the event is seen by some theologians as but the most recent example of Jewish persecution in the last two thousand years. Other scholars place Auschwitz on a level equivalent with Hiroshima, Kampuchea (Cambodia),(12) the Armenian massacre,(3) and the Stalinist reign of terror.(14) The Jewish philosopher Emil L. Fackenheim strongly disagrees with such blending of suffering. He submits that to take the suffering of a specific people at a specific point in historic time, and submerge it into the rubric of all other human suffering, is to negate and destroy the particularity of the suffering and the identity of the victims.(15)

In his new work, The Age of Triage, theologian-historian Richard L. Rubenstein has proposed a helpful context in which to see the Nazi extermination of the Jews. Rubenstein posits the Holocaust within a continuum of governmental action beginning in the Tudor period of England.(16) He attempts to demonstrate that the Holocaust is coterminous with other state-sponsored population elimination programs. When certain segments of a population are rendered superfluous or undesirable in economic or political terms, legally constituted governments have taken measures to confront the problem. Among those measures have been eviction and forced emigration, and more recently, extermination. Professor Rubenstein sees the Holocaust as the result of Germany's effort to eliminate the reservoir of Eastern European Jews who might have settled in German territory and competed for German jobs.(17) Dr. Rubenstein's perspective allows for understanding the Holocaust as a rational program -- bureaucratically administered and scientifically executed. Precisely by giving the Holocaust a meaningful context, Rubenstein has done what most other Holocaust scholars have failed to do.

By way of summary to this point,(18) we have examined a conception of the Holocaust which perceives the event as an atypical occurrence, an accident of history. This perspective does not allow Auschwitz to be interpreted as having any import for contemporary life. If it was simply an irrational outburst, a fluke, then the Holocaust can hardly be seen to have overarching significance in the formation of a worldview in 1985. The correlative to the historical accident thesis; that HaShoah is but another tragedy, albeit greater in degree; is not conducive to meaningful interpretation of the event. Though this approach does give the Holocaust a context, it does not allow for any qualitative difference in that event from any other instance of suffering and destruction.

Viewing the Holocaust as essentially like other human tragedies is exactly the point with which this author takes issue. The event was unlike other suffering not only by degree; but rather, it expanded the human conception of murder and evil outwards by several quanta. It is this author's argument that what we as members of the contemporary Western world hold to be good, and indicative of enlightened progress, had more to do with the occurrence of the Holocaust than a breakdown in social and political fabric, psychopathology, or anti-Semitism. The Holocaust becomes explicable as an event belonging to Western history in the 1940s when it is realized that its sources were among the esteemed patterns of Western thought and experience. Auschwitz and Dachau lie within the mainstream of twentieth century events as surely as the vaccine for polio, the right to vote for women in America, the United Nations enterprise, and the Civil Rights Act of 1964.(19) In short, what thought patterns and values allowed for the finest accomplishments of the modern era also made possible the worst, namely Auschwitz, the "galactic core" of the Nazi concentration camp universe. We shall attempt to argue demonstratively that nothing "went wrong" with the institutions and thought patterns of Western culture as we know them to produce the Holocaust. It can be stated that it was precisely because these patterns "went right" that the Final Solution was effective from a German standpoint. The Holocaust was not a fluke occurrence in history, but lay within the path that Enlightenment thought(20) would logically follow. In my view, the Holocaust represents a fundamental failure of direction in Western culture! It was the direction of the entire culture that went wrong, not the workings of any one institution or trend of thought therein. We all want to believe that morality necessarily followed on the footsteps of modernity. Our institutions such as universities, churches, government, and free enterprise are felt somehow to be morally positive, or at worst, morally neutral. What I see embodied in Auschwitz, however, is a synthesis of thought and institution with no moral direction. In a refreshing manner, the sociologist Ranier C. Baum postulates the primary causation of the Holocaust to be the moral indifference of the elite leaders of Germany, the politicians, professors, industrialists, and the generals.(21) "The 'best and the brightest' of German society simply did not care about the fate of Europe's Jews under National Socialism."(22) But what caused the moral indifference? Why were the Jews excluded from the German universe of moral obligation? Let us examine some of the sources that made the Endlösung possible. The combination of sources included: human intelligence, rationality, science, technology, bureaucracy, organization, capitalism, education, professionalism, humanism, legal structures,(24) modern language,(25) the concept of universal man, and the Enlightenment idea of linear progress.(26) This listing sounds like a tabulation of that which is regarded to be the best in our culture, and indeed it is! Of course it can be argued that each of the above items contributes much toward quality living. The difficulty with each, though, is the absence of internal moral guidelines and boundaries. None provide a compelling reason not to commit murder. When faced with the question of whether to participate in the murder of fellow human beings, none of the items are capable of providing one with a decisive answer. Each item places little value upon the emotional dimension in human life. Yet it is empathy, an emotional form of imagination, that permits one person to feel another person's psychological and physical pain.(27) Most significant, however, is that each element in the listing displays contempt for the transcendent or spiritual. The challenge now before us, as individuals pondering the Holocaust, is to connect that event and all of its attendant horror with these thought patterns and institutions which appear so benign and beneficial. We need to identify in what manner rationality, scientific thought, and bureaucracy, for example, directly contributed to the overall value judgments, planning, decision-making, and execution of the Final Solution.

That the Nazis were engaged in an intelligent enterprise is best demonstrated by the fact that most of the killing at institutions such as Birkenau, Maidanek, and Treblinka was done largely in a detached manner, without malice or hatred displayed towards the victims. The thousands of people who were being murdered day after day had ceased to be part of the human family; they had become abstractions. A well-organized bureaucratic system such as the National Socialists developed for dehumanizing and killing Jews could not have been sustained for twelve years on the adrenalin of hatred. Deep-seated theological and cultural anti-Semitism may have allowed the Nazi hierarchy to initially select the Jews as the prototype of those people to be destroyed. However, it was rational, well-integrated procedures which had to have followed through with the execution process. The Final Solution was the result of the application of human intelligence and rational analysis to a perceived problem. Intelligence was used to organize the suffering. Consider the following if you will: There was a substantial European and Soviet Jewish population which in the minds of many had to be erased. Imagine the complexity and logistics of registering, transporting, and coordinating the movement of millions of people over thousands of miles. Literally thousands of statisticians, clerks, accountants, typists, train engineers, and station managers -- bureaucrats and civil servants at every level. Think of all the planning, designing, and engineering involved in such a massive enterprise, with each person carrying his own small portion of the Endlösung der Judenfrage. The Final Solution was indeed a machine run on rational tracks.

Direct evidence of scientific activity in the concentration camp system comes from the medical experiments at Auschwitz and other camps.(28) German physicians trained long before Hitler's ascension to power at some of Europe's finest medical schools conducted experiments on Jewish men, women, and children. Medical and scientific ethics supposedly transmitted through the education process of those professional schools proved to be irrelevant. The thirst for technical and professional competence and new knowledge evidently guided the activities of such men as Dr. Josef Mengele. Unlike a normal laboratory setting wherein knowledge learned from animal studies is cautiously applied to human beings; at Auschwitz, doctors and technicians had human patients for their analyses. No longer did data and conclusions have to be overcast by the dubious extrapolation from a point lower on the phylogenetic tree(29) to man himself. It is interesting to note that eminent German physicians accepted the results of research conducted on Jewish people, despite that Jews were legally defined to be Untermensch, "subhuman", and presented in popular propaganda as vermin. Obviously, socio-political definitions did not stand in the way of scientific inquiry. Though science may not have been directly involved in the categorization of Jews as undesirable, it nonetheless made use of the human members of such delineation.(30) Some of Germany's largest industries, such as the I.G. Farben,(31) had their products tested on camp inmates. Among the products evaluated was a treatment for phosphorus burns. To observe the effectiveness of this remedy, the patient, or rather unwilling victim, had to be subjected to chemical burning. In American high school and college biology labs, a frog is at least pithed to destroy its brain prior to experimentation.(32) Yet not even local anesthetic was used during forced castrations and hysterectomies performed at Auschwitz.

We can see evidence of scientific methodology at work in the perfecting of the killing process. In order to reach the epitome in technically advanced killing symbolized by the Birkenau complex at Auschwitz, the Nazis had to proceed through a series of intermediate phases -- experimental steps. The object of the experiment was to engineer a system whereby thousands of people could be killed each day in a cost-effective, psychologically painless mechanism. Beginning in the late 1930s with a euthanasia program originally designed for mentally and physically handicapped Germans, the killing process went through such phases as mobile death squads and carbon monoxide gas vans to permanent locations wherein carbon monoxide and prussic acid were utilized. The outcome of this joint effort of science, bureaucracy, and industry was the bloodless death factory.

The application of rationality to production, which had allowed for the onset of mass production in industry, was integrated into the death camp in a similar way.(33) Raw materials that included human beings and their possessions were processed in assembly-line fashion complete with production quotas and reports until a final product, corpse or ash, was produced and disposed of. Imagine all of the possessions, the many inventory clerks, and the people involved in the transport and marketing of those items.

Of course engineers were needed to design concentration camp sites and crematoria. Bids and contracts were naturally involved, with the necessity for lawyers and cost accountants. Direct involvement of the capitalist enterprise in the Final Solution is most apparent in the industrial exploitation of Jewish victims. Businessman and accountants from several large, German-based firms found Jewish slave labor(34) very economically attractive. The Farben conglomerate, for example, realized the capitalist utopia that was the concentration camp.(35) Farben made heavy investments in establishing synthetic oil and rubber installations at Auschwitz. This cartel also built the concentration camp called Monowitz (Auschwitz IV) to house the slave labor supply for its factories. Traditional labor problems were very much reduced because the concentration camp allowed for marginal labor costs to the firm, forced productivity, and a large supply of workers. The limits to profit could be pursued with a vengeance. One must ask the question: What is the moral posture of capitalist ideology? Reaping the benefits of Nazi political maneuvers regarding the status of the Jews, German industry displayed a clear model of what capitalism might become. The utilization of the Jews as an expendable machine or draft animal reflects a twentieth century motif in human interpretation -- man the machine or doer, as opposed to man the thinker and feeler. The age of the machine has brought with it the universal re-evaluation of all entities in terms of utility, productivity, and efficiency. Such perspective allows no place for a cognitive-emotional image of the human being. Furthermore, it is easier to enslave, torture, and kill a machine than it is to kill a person who is perceived in a human context.

I would like to reintroduce a thought mentioned previously in the discussion of intelligence, namely, the perception of the Jews as <u>abstractions</u>. Such conception was necessary to initially place the Jew outside any framework of moral obligation. This perception needed to be maintained in order for the entire killing network to remain intact and functioning in a business-as-usual manner. This author argues that the origin of the notion of Jew as abstraction and the force which insured its maintenance are to be found in the prevailing scientific mentality(36) of the modern era. This scientific approach has appropriated rationality, reason, and intellect as its own. The very foundations of human progress in the post-Enlightenment period are thus inextricably linked with science.(37) Let us examine some of the components of scientific methodology, beginning with intelligence. When intelligence is measured psychologically, what is being evaluated is one's ability to manipulate non-concrete entities, in effect, abstractions. The same abstract capacity that allows one to mentally picture and manipulate electrons, and thereby understand electronics, also permits one to treat people as interchangeable figures on a business ledger or speak of several million people out of work as 10.8 percent of the work force unemployed. Of course we must make use of our intelligence to accomplish goals most efficiently. The choice of goals, however, lies in the realm of values. The German elite had the empirical knowledge(38) to formulate prussic acid,(39) but to apply that product in the extermination of rodents or human beings was a value judgment. The same intellect and scientific "know-how" which produced this chemical did not provide any direction for its use in morally sound channels. Within the framework of Nazi thinking, the Jews of Europe became the problem in a scientific paradigm; and as such, they were removed from any human context. On a popular level, Jews were transformed into abstract problems by such forces as state-sponsored propaganda, scientifically formulated racial theories, value-free scientific language, and anti-Jewish sentiment. The Final Solution to the Jewish problem could then be accomplished with the application of a chemical; without an excess of psychological stress or moral indignation on the part of the killers. The killers could even call themselves humane! They had analyzed the problem and arrived at a <u>reasonable</u> solution. The philosopher Max Horkheimer's commentary on human reason is appropriate here. "In lay discussion as well as in scientific, reason has come to be commonly regarded as an intellectual faculty of co-ordination, the efficiency of which can be increased by methodical use and by the removal of any non-intellectual factors, such as conscious or unconscious emotions. Reason has never really directed social reality, but now reason has been so thoroughly purged of any specific trend or preference that it has finally renounced even the task of passing judgment on man's actions and way of life."(40) To exhibit reason, therefore, is to act in a non-emotional, non-subjective, value-free manner. To be reasonable is to be objective and non-judgmental. <u>By not engaging in value judgments, reasonable people allow society to proceed in a business-as-usual manner.</u>(41)

Rationality is the last element we will note with respect to scientific methodology. Rationality is a way of doing things, a means, whereby reality is understood and contemplated in terms of thought and reason, overagainst "emotion, intuition, or extra-sensory modes of apprehension."(42) Because the methodology of science is premised upon the intellect, reason, and rationality, it therefore is morally directionless. Science per se has no intrinsic source of values; there are no built-in control mechanisms to direct the course of science away from morally reprehensible actions. Science can be applied as easily to the establishment of an Auschwitz as to the development of an artificial heart. Though science possesses no essential values, this is not to infer that it does not alter existing values and create new ones of its own design. This author is prepared to argue that the pervasiveness of scientific mentality has fundamentally altered the limits of human behavior, the general concept of human beings, and the entire direction of Western culture. The Holocaust should be seen lying squarely within the path in which scientific mentality has directed the modern era. Scientific knowledge about human beings simply does not provide any sufficient rationale to treat people humanely in the traditional religious conception of humaneness. Science talks in terms of people being not more than bodies in which certain chemical and electrical processes occur. The human mind, because it cannot yet be quantified, is often considered to be a black box. The Skinnerian school of behavioral psychology holds that the mind is such a black box. In this model, the mind is reduced to an integrator of stimuli and responses.(43) The only facets of anything which science will consider are those which are empirically verifiable. Death, in scientific motif, can be reduced to an increase in the entropy of the carbon atom configuration that is popularly referred to as a human being. This concept of death, and ones similar to it, do not encourage that human life be given any priority. What does mother, father, child, or neighbor mean in the scheme of science wherein there is essentially "contemplation devoid of all interest".(44) If all people are simply electro-chemical processes and carbon-hydrogen bonds, then human relationships, commitments, and responsibilities are meaningless. It follows that if people are only chemical processes, then "there can be neither qualitative nor quantitative distinction drawn between loss of life by one means or another."(45) Yet life is not homogenous, therefore why should death be considered so? The entire concept of values is based on the affirmation that there <u>are</u> differences in reality. To die as a soldier or a hapless civilian caught in a bombing are fundamentally distinct from being purposefully sought and murdered because of who one is. How can we talk of values and priorities if all things are conceptually equal? Life itself then has no value!

We might pause to consider the direction these arguments are taking us. Many readers might ask: Is not science essentially neutral on moral issues? Does not science comprise but one of many ways of looking at reality? Is it not <u>society</u>'s <u>role</u> to guide the application of scientific innovation? How could science, which deals with unbiased facts, be implicated in the killing of millions of people?, and then not only implicated in the physical destruction process, but also in the mental decision-making process which led people to commit such crimes. Are not science and rationality intellectual "demilitarized zones" wherein reality can be examined in a clear light, unencumbered by religion, emotion, or historical context?

At this point we may be able to see how thinking, educated, reasonable people participated in the Final Solution. It was not that these people stopped thinking, buried their education, or became unreasonable. Rather, the scientific Zeitgeist(46) of the modern era had largely dictated how to think. The scientific mode of inquiry had been expanded beyond the limits of being only an institution; it is now a part of the basic fabric of society just as the Church once was part of that basic fabric.(47) The thought of the Swedish playwright August Strindberg is profound on this very point. "A generation that had the courage to get rid of God, to crush the state and the church, and to overthrow society and morality, still bowed before Science."(48) Scientific methodology is not just apparent in chemistry and biology, but what were once termed humanities(49) are now known as social science and political science. We also have the phenomenon of scientific creationism. Even fundamentalist religion recognizes the stamp of authority that science lends to one's cause. This single pattern of thinking espoused by scientific rationality colored, in large part, the decisions of the educated German elite regarding European Jews. We should now ask: Why have the conceptual tools of scientific rationality (abstraction, emotionlessness, value-free judgment) become accepted as the authoritative means of knowing anything about reality? The scholar George G. Iggers marks the emergence of rationality as the dominant way of looking at reality in the eighteenth century Enlightenment period.(50) Several philosophers including Ludwig Wittgenstein and Paul K. Feyerabend have suggested that our selection of science as the means of knowing, over and above non-rational means (such as religion and emotion), was an arbitrary act.(51) What these scholars are postulating is that scientific rationality(52) is only one tradition of interpreting reality. To choose science above all else is arbitrary, in effect, not based on any absolute intrinsic value in science. Science itself would disclaim any absolutes upon which to premise such a choice. We have come to assume that emotion, pure thought, myth, and human spirituality yield faulty perceptions when applied to understanding life in general. Over the past two hundred fifty years, science has risen to prominence by making the religious perspective appear meaningless. Religion was the primary obstacle to the ascension of modern science. Rather than serving as one tradition among many, scientific rationality is now the standard to which other traditions must conform.(53) Science as a means of knowing about reality effaces all other alternatives. The author Antoine De Saint-Exupery has something of significance to tell us here.

> If you were to say to grown-ups: 'I saw a beautiful house made of rosy brick, with geraniums in the windows and doves on the roof' they would not be able to get any idea of the house at all. You would have to say to them: 'I saw a house that cost $20,000.' Then they would exclaim: "Oh, what a pretty house that is!'
>
> Just so, you might say to them: 'The proof that the little prince existed is that he was charming, that he laughed, and that he was looking for a sheep... .' And what good would it do to tell them that? They would shrug their shoulders, and treat you like a child.(54)

This passage from the classic, The Little Prince, may serve to illustrate that reality can be legitimately perceived and comprehended in diametrical ways. The confinement of knowledge about the house to its twenty thousand dollar cost is only one means of knowing about it. The tendency given critique in The Little Prince is the adult or mature conception which discounts seemingly subjective descriptions of reality and accepts only objective fact -- the cost.

I would not be so concerned with the mentality of science were it not for its pervasiveness. If science were competing in the "marketplace of ideas",(55) the impact of its attendant mentality would necessarily be blunted. Yet, after Buchenwald and Dachau, the import of such mentality has not abated; but rather, it has accentuated. We now live in a more intensely technical era than forty years ago. What is it I see that should concern us about this state of affairs? At the risk of being termed a contemporary Cassandra,(56) I will expand upon my concerns. By presenting the problems I see with scientific mentality, I am not arguing from the standpoint of naturalism.(57) It is not my attempt to be anti-intellectual by demonstrating the dangers of science and technology.(58) I am pragmatic enough to recognize that "the advance of modern science will not be stopped, even if some of its theories should turn out to be mistaken... ."(59) My efforts, therefore, are not to effect the return to a simpler era. Rather, I am pointing out the problems of scientific mentality precisely because it constitutes the epicenter of the modern worldview to the exclusion of all else.(60) From my perspective, science acts as a kind of cultural abrasive, flattening out ethnic, religious, and personal contours and particularity. In our scientific milieu, identification with ethnic or religious distinction is often viewed as clinging to hollow tradition. A group such as the Association of Orthodox Jewish Scientists, for example, would appear to many people to be a contradiction in terms. The whole notion of tradition is largely discounted in our modern era. This is not to argue that traditions should not be questioned, but it is myopic to discount them as without meaning simply because they cannot be demonstrated valid by empirical means. Cultural flattening, or social homogenization, was an objective of National Socialism and remains on the social agenda of most modern political states.(61) Scientific thinking contributed to such homogeneity by rendering social and traditional differences anachronistic.(62)

Science has rendered structureless the moral framework that was held in place by religion. Traditional values and ethics premised upon divine revelation have fallen before the scientific viewpoint. The French scholar Jacques Monod asserts that science may indeed be more destructive in terms of ideas and concepts it nullifies than in physical terms such as the atomic bomb.(63) That science has destroyed ideas may be more dangerous than the nuclear threat science has helped to create. Science has eroded the meaningfulness of the religious perspective by developing its own cosmology, for example. The evolution of life on earth and the origins of the universe are two areas which we will develop to demonstrate specifically how science undercut the religious perspective. Genetic research shows that by using selective breeding methods, plants or animals with specific phenotypic(64) characteristics can be produced. Such evidence argues strongly for the evolutionary theory of development. The Russian scientist Oparin has demonstrated that organic material (proteins) can be made from inorganic, inert elements. Under specific conditions, then, <u>life</u> (proteins, nucleic acids) can derive from only inorganic material. The biblical concept of Creation is thus severely challenged. The biological models of genetic recombination and mutation (occurring over time) can explain the development of life on earth with no appeal to Deity. The origin of the universe is also explained in part by the scientific theory of the Big Bang. According to this theory, at some point in time, there was monumental explosion of matter which gave rise to the stars, planets, asteroids, etc. Because science's views are subject to verification in an objective sense, they are more accepted than faith statements and models of reality involving G-d. It is apparent that the white lab coat has become the sacred garb of the modern world.(65) Concurrently, "technology is...the source of salvation, the agent of secularized redemption; technological advance is...secularized eschatology."(66) In place of morality based upon obeying G-d's commandments or emulating Christ,(67) scientific rationality tries to create universal moral imperatives. Such secular imperatives certainly did not function in a compulsory manner from 1933-45. Secular humanism somehow assumes that human life is important. Why? Because people are an interesting life form? What <u>compelling</u> rationale does science or humanism offer for not killing? In what way is life to derive value because of science? The social ethicist John T. Pawlikowski correctly contends that "the threat before us is...ovens and gas chambers manned by those who would claim to have the ultimate replacement for the religious perspective."(68) Social systems analyst Jay W. Forrester, whose writing reflects a very secular, rational, modern spirit, nevertheless maintains that there is a legitimate and necessary place for religion in the present and the future. Professor Forrester asserts that "there is no custodian of the long-term goals unless it be the religious institutions. On religion rests the responsibility for maintaining long-term values and preventing the collapse of operating goals."(69) Dr. Forrester sees organized religion as having the longest time horizon,(70) in effect, being concerned with the distant future. By virtue of its future time perspective, religion can act to keep society on a path consistent with long-term goals. In fairness to science, the displacement of the religious perspective by scientific rationality did not result in social chaos.(71) Yet, utopia was not the outcome either.

Another problem I see with a general scientific orientation in society is that the "checks and balances system" which theoretically exists between society and scientific innovation becomes a dangerous illusion. Science supposedly relies upon society to put its findings to use in moral ways. Yet science has rendered meaningless the foundations for any countervailing morality. Our record as a society insofar as the cautious application of scientific innovation is highly suspect when we consider nuclear power, for example. "In the technologically oriented culture of today, it is difficult if not impossible to exercise caution once a technology has been developed."(72) Because of the prevailing scientific outlook, life is perceived in the "problem-goal" paradigm. The alternatives for solving the "problems" are also provided by science. Example: the Soviet Union is perceived as the "problem" facing the Western world. Our alternatives for "solving" this "problem" are not predominantly intercultural or intra-human exchanges and bridge-building. Rather, our solutions are high-technology warheads.

Even if this "checks and balances system" were intact, "our ever-growing scientific mastery over the forces of nature imposes an almost unbearable responsibility on political authority and on a democratic electorate to learn about, think about, plan for, and use these forces for real human benefit."(73) Elected representatives and the general public can hardly expect to grasp the technical meaning of current research, much less comprehend the social impact. The symbiosis of science and the modern political state(74) makes the social control of technology problematic. Standing up against the application of scientific research that is state-supported takes on the stigma of disloyalty or lack of patriotism. The futurist Robert Jungk strongly believes that "technology can no longer be seen as a neutral force but must be seen as one which is dependent on political and economic power groups whose concepts of things to come largely preempt the future and shape the world of tomorrow before the young, who will have to live in that world, can have any say in these decisions."(75) Instead of in parliaments and congresses, decisions are made in think tanks and research and development departments.(76) The specific research that is receiving funding from government and industry today will determine what is feasible and available twenty or thirty years from now.

To this point, we have examined some of the problems of a pervasive scientific mentality: the erosion of tradition and human identity, the fragmentation of the moral framework provided by religion, and the ineffectiveness of a checks and balances system on scientific innovation. We will now examine several other problems with our science-centered Western culture. Education is no longer conducted in a pluralistic setting. There are, to be sure, historical and sociological methodologies. However, all modern educational methodologies emulate the scientific pattern. The direction in the humanities and social-behavioral sciences is towards quantitative, rational analysis. Paul K. Feyerabend correctly maintains that education does not involve a mere presentation of physical (astronomical, biological, sociological) facts and principles. One does not learn: some people believe the earth moves around the sun; rather one learns: the earth moves around the sun -- with the implication that everything else is nonsense!(77) It is noteworthy that scientific programs have been the ones to receive the most funding over the last twenty-five years in American public schools. Let's consider this: the elite leaders of Nazi Germany, exposed to the scientific thrust of the educational system, could be expected to be inclined to think in scientific-rational channels rather than predominantly religious-emotional paths. What concerns me now is the specter of politically-appointed bureaucrats in our Pentagon, educated in the scientific regimen, raised in the rationalist, modern spirit, who make judgments involving billions of dollars and millions of lives without a sense of the Transcendent. Values based upon transcendent respect for human beings remain exogenous to their decision-making.

Scientific methods and thinking, be they in the form of physics, history, or psychology, have been established as the predominant, if not sole, tradition in education.(78) No other tradition, no other theory of knowledge, has access to the power represented in state-supported education as does science. It is not surprising that our schools produce technically competent professionals capable of value-free decision-making. The whole scientific approach is to excise any non-intellectual factors such as conscious or unconscious emotions from an analysis.(79) Bertrand Russell's admonition that "we know too much and feel too little"(80) is an accurate assessment of the results of education conducted according to scientific rationalism. The sociologist Dr. Katz has remarked that we do not know enough about such heinous crimes as the Holocaust to prevent them.(81) I submit that knowledge alone will not serve as an effective deterrent to another Holocaust. People must cultivate feeling, and with it, empathy. Knowledge, no matter how refined and in-depth, is not going to be enough.

The Holocaust should emerge from this discussion as an understandable part of mainstream twentieth century culture. The event is of the culture, not above it on a metahistorical plane nor below it in a demonic abyss. With the combination of contempt for transcendent values that comes from scientific rationalism and contempt for the material world that comes from centuries of Christian theology, there can be mass death. When we realize that barbaric actions can be committed by rational, educated, Westernized people precisely because they are rational, we might come closer to grasping the reality of HaShoah. In modern times, we no longer are threatened by marauding hordes of barbaric horsemen. We now have governmental departments and agencies armed with scientific expertise to expedite the killing of population segments. It is extraordinarily difficult for one to not become cynical and bitter with this state of affairs. It is quite disconcerting, and indeed frightening, to perceive one's way of life as being the source of total domination and extermination of a people. The Western way of life is introduced and reinforced via parents, schools, churches, legislatures, and courts to name only several. What will serve to invest Western institutions with humaneness and with sensitivity to human capacity, concerns, and direction? It would certainly appear doubtful whether the same institutions that would have predicted that the Holocaust could never have occurred where and when it did would be helpful in this quest.(82) The Holocaust altered reality in a fundamental way. Life and our perception of it can never be the same. Our task is to imagine, create, and consolidate human-oriented alternatives to the manner in which we conduct business, educate our young people, govern, and administer law. The Holocaust demands our involvement and our interest in efforts to develop specific pathways of response to this most dis-orienting historical experience.

The Image of Man: An Essay

Man is a machine, a statement absurd to some people and lived by others. Upon close review of human qualities and activities, I found many of these activities duplicated by the machine, yet Jewish convictions tell me machines are not men. I must search for differences between men and mechanical devices to reinforce those convictions.

Perhaps the ego would serve well as the initial difference between man and machine. A machine's being, its existence, is not known to itself. The concept of self is absent, and thus the machine has no identity to seek or to preserve. Although self is not present in the mechanical device, it does possess a predictability that is frustratingly missing in human beings. When one sets or programs a mechanical device to behave in a specific manner, the machine responds in accordance with its programming. On the other hand, a football coach, for example, can teach an athlete to react in a particular way to a given defensive formation and yet observe a totally opposite response to the situation in the game. A man's actions are not to be extrapolated from previous responses and conditioning.

Consequently, a man is capable of coping with and adapting to conditions to which he has never before been exposed. Derived from his ability to think, these faculties allow man to take what he knows and apply that to the situation at hand. A human being, unlike a machine, can thus live with such happenings as the death of a friend or total financial failure. Coupled with thought is man's distinctive ability to reason; and therefore, the capacity and the opportunity of making choices. Man has alternatives: of an intellectual or emotional response to a problem, of right or wrong, of an occupation, of a religion. A man can take from his surroundings those entities which will have meaning and utility for himself; a machine must merely digest the information fed into it. Man can make his own world.

Yet man is not bound by his surroundings. He can escape from the present state of being through his imagination. Unlike the machine which must exist in the realm of facts, data, and physical limitations, man can cross into the world of fantasy. A man can dream far beyond the limits of actual fulfillment.

Returning to the realm of reality...a man is able to learn things by himself. Not confined to parasitic existence, a man is capable of discovery from the early days of his childhood. A machine can detect things and occurrences, but it cannot appreciate them or know satisfaction from them as a man can. Man is not restricted to the level of physical sensation, (such as sight, taste, and hearing), but is able to feel deep emotion. A man can hate, be afraid, and love, and experience the subsequent dwarfing and revitalization from each. A man can laugh and feel the mirth beneath his smile...I say a man has feelings.

Finally, the most salient difference between man and machine is that men were created by G-d, whereas machines were made by men. G-d is infinitely more creative, trusting and purposeful than to merely manufacture robot creatures. Machines are totally in the earthly realm; man comes from the divine and possesses divinity in his soul.

NOTES

CHAPTER V

THE HOLOCAUST, SCIENTIFIC RATIONALITY,
AND TRANSCENDENCE:
CRITIQUE AND SYNTHESIS

1. George M. Kren and Leon Rappoport, "Failures of Thought in Holocaust Interpretation," mimeographed, p. 7.

2. Cognitive dissonance is a psychological term referring to the attempt of one person to believe two conflicting ideas at the same time. In post-Copernican times, for example, persons who accepted a geocentric universe on theological terms had to attempt to mesh this belief with the astronomical observation that the earth was not the center of the universe. The attempt to mesh religious belief and scientific theory has been a source of much cognitive dissonance in the post-Enlightenment period.

3. Die Ausrottung translates from the German as "destruction, extirpation, or eradication".

4. L'holocauste is the French rendition of Holocaust.

5. Kren and Rappoport, "Failures of Thought," p. 8.

6. Ibid., p. 9.

7. Social, economic, and political stress in pre-World War II Germany:

The conditions set forth in the Treaty of Versailles (1919) after the First World War are often interpreted as factors which would help explain the rise of Adolf Hitler to power. First, this treaty was negotiated without German representation. Specific points of the treaty included: German acceptance of reparation payments, German restoration of the provinces of Alsace and Lorraine to France, cession of the majority of West Prussia to Poland, placement of the German colonies under League of Nations' mandate, limitation of German military strength, and provision for Allied occupation of the Rhineland. However, it must also be stated that the war itself, lasting from 1914 to 1918, left the German nation in economic ruin. It cannot be validly maintained that the whole of Germany's social and economic problems after 1918 were externally imposed.

The Weimar government, which was established in 1919 under President Ebert, was plagued with gross unemployment and inflation from the outset. Following a short period of economic revitalization around 1925, Germany was once again in times of severe social and economic stress with the onset of the Great Depression in 1929. Concurrently, Adolf Hitler's NSDAP was the largest single political party in the Reichstag (German parliament) by 1929. Hitler was appointed chancellor of Germany by Paul von Hindenburg in January of 1933.

An example of explaining the German public's participation in and silence to the Holocaust in terms of social stress is found in the writing of Norman Cohn. "Particularly in periods of exceptional strain, anxiety, and disorientation, multitudes of people yielded to the temptation to blame all their trouble on the ... (Jew) ... -- reacting to social and economic crises, for instance, very much as their ancestors had reacted to the plague." "The Myth of the Jewish World-Conspiracy: A Case Study in Collective Psychopathology," Commentary 41(1966): 42.

8. The actions of individuals in the German extermination program are often interpreted as uncritical obedience to authority. The S.S., camp guards, and even the Nazi administrators all claimed to have been "only following orders" in carrying out their "duty". See the commentary on psychologist Stanley Milgram's famous experiment, "Some Conditions of Obedience and Disobedience to Authority", in Chester A. Insko and John Schopler, Experimental Social Psychology, pp. 327-43. Milgram's observations of human behavior in a laboratory setting have been applied to actions of the Nazi murderers.

The S.S. or Schutzstaffel was under the command of Heinrich Himmler. Most S.S. men belonged to the Allgemeine SS (General SS), though there also was the Totenkopfverbände (Death's Head Units) and Waffen-SS (Armed SS). For more on the S.S., see Lucy S. Dawidowicz, The War Against the Jews 1933-1945, pp. 98-102; Helmut Crausnick and Martin Broszat, The Anatomy of the SS State; and Heinz Höhne, The Order of the Deathshead.

9. Kren and Rappoport, "Failure of Thought," p. 9.

10. The Jewish affirmation and commitment to remember the Holocaust constitutes precisely what George M. Kren and Leon Rappoport see as the submersion of meaning into explanation. "Remember the Holocaust" means that the more we know about the event from an historical, sociological, and psychological perspective, the less likely it is to recur.

11. *Totalitarianism*, ([total] + author [itarian]), is a system of domination wherein a government enforces monolithic unity among a population by authoritarian means. In totalitarianism, there is a total assault on the human personality; there is an attempt to control the individual from within. See also Hannah Arendt and George Orwell.

12. Kampuchea (formerly Cambodia in Southeast Asia) was the site of mass murders from 1975-1979 under the regime headed by Pol Pot. Following Pol Pot's vision of a peasant nation, the Khmer Rouge communists forced the inhabitants of Phnom Penh and other Cambodian cities and towns into the countryside. There, the educated class, deemed to be tainted by Western influence, was executed. The remainder of the urban population was incarcerated in work camps and given few provisions with which to live. The total estimate of the number of people killed in those five years is two to three million. See Peter T. White, "Kampuchea Wakens from a Nightmare," *National Geographic*, May 1982, pp. 590-622; and Richard L. Rubenstein, "The Agony of Indochina," in *The Age of Triage*, pp. 165-94.

13. The Armenian massacre occurred during World War I. It was a "deliberate decision taken by the Turkish Government ... to transform Turkish society by means of the systematic extermination of Turkey's Armenian Christian population ...." Rubenstein, *Age of Triage*, p. 12. See also, Michael J. Arlen, *Passage to Ararat*.

14. Joseph Stalin's attempt to place Soviet agriculture under state control (collectivization) is estimated to have cost twenty-one million lives. See Aleksandr Solzhenitsyn, *The Gulag Archipelago, 1918-1956*.

15. Emil L. Fackenheim, "Jewish Faith and the Holocaust: *A Fragment*," *Commentary* 46(1968): 30.

16. The Tudor period in England refers to the time during which the royal Tudor family ruled that country, namely, from 1485-1603. The House of Stuart succeeded the Tudor dynasty on the death of Elizabeth in 1603.

17. Rubenstein's thoughts on the Holocaust were heard at the Eighth Annual Conference on the Holocaust held in Philadelphia in October, 1982. See also, Rubenstein, "The Unmasked Trauma: The Elimination of the European Jews," in Age of Triage, pp. 128-64. It should be noted that the Nazis' initial effort at elimination of the Jews was to force them to emigrate. However, other nations chose not to accept the Jews of Europe in any great numbers.

18. Because of my discussion of theological interpretations of the Holocaust in two other chapters, I will not discuss those themes here.

19. Several scholars and theologians also assert that the Holocaust was a rational event lying in the mainstream of Western culture: Richard L. Rubenstein, The Cunning of History, p. 21; Rubenstein, Age of Triage; George M. Kren and Leon Rappoport, The Holocaust and the Crisis of Human Behavior; Henry Friedlander, "Toward a Methodology of Teaching about the Holocaust," Teachers College Record 80(1979): 520; John T. Pawlikowski, The Challenge of the Holocaust for Christian Theology, p. 3; John T. Pawlikowski, "The Holocaust as Rational Event," Reconstructionist 40(1974): 8; and Henry L. Feingold, "Who Shall Bear Guilt for the Holocaust: The Human Dilemma," American Jewish History 68(1979): 266.

20. The Enlightenment period of history involved a significant shift in thought and perception about the world. Previously accepted doctrines and institutions; most notable concerning the Church, governmental structures, and the concept of the nature of man; were subjected to examination from the point of view of rationalism. The Enlightenment was a liberal, humanitarian, and scientific trend of thought which, to a certain extent, was translated into such social actions as the American Revolution (1775) and the French Revolution (1789). The Enlightenment viewpoint was given expression in the writings of Jean Jacques Rousseau and Voltaire (France), David Hume (England), Thomas Paine (America), Gotthold Lessing and Immanuel Kant (Germany), and Cesare Beccaria (Italy). The English philosopher John Locke (1632-1704) is regarded to have

provided much in the way of philosophical foundation for the Enlightenment.

21. See Ranier C. Baum, The Holocaust and the German Elite.

22. Warren K. A. Thompson's review of Ranier C. Baum, The Holocaust and the German Elite, Business and Professional Ethics Journal 2(1982): 85.

23. Universe of obligation was borrowed from a lecture delivered by the Israeli historian Yehuda Bauer at the Eighth Annual Conference on the Holocaust held in Philadelphia in October of 1982.

24. Certainly law did not control human behavior or effect any humanitarian ethos in the 1930s and 1940s. The Hitler government was duly and legally installed into office; it was voted into power. That government effected the Nuremberg Laws of 1935 through legitimate legal procedure. Those laws deprived German Jews of many of their civil rights. It should also be noted that genocide was not even a defined crime prior to 1945. The crimes against humanity committed under the auspices of the Nazi elite were made crimes only after the fact. Murder was, of course, a legally defined crime prior to 1945. Laws against murder as a state-sponsored program have little chance of enforcement, however. One must also consider how just punishment under the law can be administered against persons responsible for the death and suffering of hundreds of thousands of people. In effect, how is the murder of five people to be punished differently than the murder of five thousand?

In addition, the democratic process in America did not respond to the desperate needs of the Jews of Europe. One effective avenue of response would have been the relaxation of immigration laws that established strict nation-by-nation quotas. In the case of these immigration laws, legal structures operated against any humanitarian concerns.

25. The Nazis utilized language in its modern neutered form to refer euphemistically to actions such as the deportation, ghettoization, and murder of human beings. It has been suggested that such value-free language as the Nazis employed; words such as "special handling", "Final Solution", and "special action"; rather than reflecting real events, actually determined the way people administering the extermination program

viewed those events. Instead of language following from reality; reality was refracted through the medium of language. See Kren and Rappoport, Holocaust and Crisis of Behavior, p. 137.

26. Man as a complete human being -- mentally, emotionally, and morally -- has not accomplished linear progress in the Enlightenment connotation of the word progress. Belief in man's steady improvement on a societal scale contributed to disbelief and lack of reaction to the reality of the Jewish situation in Europe.

27. Richard L. Means, The Ethical Imperative, p. 145.

28. In connection with the medical experiments conducted at Auschwitz, see Milos Nyislzi, Auschwitz; Raul Hilberg, The Destruction of the European Jews, pp. 600-09; and Robert Jay Lifton, "Medicalized Killing in Auschwitz," Psychiatry 45(1982): 283-97.

29. Phylogenetic tree, a biological term, refers to the arrangement of organisms according to their evolutionary development. A test animal such as a frog would occupy a lower position on the phylogenetic tree as compared to man.

30. The medical community in the United States has used prison inmates as subjects to conduct experiments such as skin grafting and pharmaceutical testing. Technically, the inmates were volunteers, yet, the lure of a reduced prison sentence or consideration at time of parole may have been used as leverage to gain compliance. Such leverage would not have been operable on the average citizen. Thus, prison inmates are perceived by the scientific community as a pool of human guinea pigs to test in ways not permissible on the general public. Though science does not necessarily create the categories of people (prisoner and free citizen), it will utilize people who have been segregated from the general public as subjects for questionable experimentation. See James H. Jones, Bad Blood. This volume details the venereal disease experimentation conducted on Southern blacks from 1932 to 1972 under the auspices of the United States Public Health Service. Jones draws specific parallels between the Nazi medical experiments and those of the U.S. Public Health Service. See also, Robert Gomer, John V. Powell, and Bert V. A. Röling, "Japan's Biological Weapons: 1930-1945," Bulletin of the Atomic Scientists

37(1981): 43-53. This article discusses Japan's use of prisoners of war in testing biological weapons. In exchange for immunity from prosecution as war criminals, the Japanese military and medical elite turned over the scientific data generated from such human experimentation to the United States government. "National security" took precedence over legality and morality. More than one legally constituted government, therefore, has perpetrated and made use of unethical medical experiments conducted on unwilling and/or unknowing human victims. Such a phenomenon is not indigenous to Germany!

31. It should be noted that the I.G. Farben (Interessen gemeinschaft Farbenindustrie Aktiengesellschaft) was an international cartel, and not only a German industry. Interessen gemeinschaft means "community of interest". The cartel included a major dyestuffs industry, operations for the production of synthetic nitrates for fertilizers, and Bayer pharmaceuticals. In America, the I.G. was intimately associated with some of the largest corporations including Dupont Chemical, Dow Chemical, and Standard Oil of New Jersey. See Joseph Brokin, The Crime and Punishment of I.G. Farben.

32. Pithing involves the insertion of a needle into the brain of the frog to destroy sensory integration capacities, and hence to prevent pain.

33. The statement linking rationality with mass production was borrowed from Rubenstein, Age of Triage, p. 5.

34. On the topic of Jewish slave labor, see Benjamin B. Ferencz, Less Than Slaves.

35. For additional information on industrial exploitation, see Rubenstein, "Health Professions and the Corporate Enterprise at Auschwitz," in Cunning of History, pp. 48-67; and Hilberg, Destruction of European Jews, pp. 586-600.

The modern importance of capitalism is related to the Industrial Revolution (c. 1750-1850). The revolution marked the transition from an agrarian and craft economy to industrialism, with the subsequent sharp delineation between the owner class and labor. Capitalism is characterized by profit drive and private ownership of property. Several pervasive notions derive from industrialism. First is the mechanized view of man, which results in part from the assembly-line procedures of industry. Man is measured by his productivity; he is but another resource. Because of its desire for profit maximization, corporate capitalism sees the situation of workers costing little in return for their time and skill as a utopia. See David S. Landes, The Unbound Prometheus. Dr. Landes is professor of history at Harvard University.

It could be argued that the presence of the I.G. Farben at Auschwitz was, in fact, instrumental in saving some Jews from immediate death. Slave labor may have provided some people with a reason to live. At least they felt themselves to be of some minute utility to the Nazis; such feeling breeds hope, however dim.

36. For another analysis of the importation of scientific mentality vis-a-vis the Holocaust, see Kren and Rappoport, "The Holocaust and the Human Condition," in Holocaust and Crisis of Behavior, pp. 125-43.

37. A synopsis linking progress, science, and rationality is as follows: Progress in the modern sense is thought of largely in terms of scientific and technical achievement. In turn, scientific advance is premised upon a mentality that espouses rationality and reason.

38. Empirical analysis refers to learning about reality from observation, experiment, experience, and sensory contact.

39. Prussic acid, marketed as Zyklon B, was originally intended for use as a rodenticide and fumigant.

40. Max Horkheimer, Eclipse of Reason, pp. 8-9.

41. The notion that reason supports conformity to reality as it is, in effect, the status quo, was borrowed from Ibid., p. 10.

42. Landes, Unbound Prometheus, p. 21.

43. In science, when something is quantified it has been precisely measured according to established modes of analysis. A process is quantified when it can be understood in mathematical terms. No adequate mathematical model has been proposed to explain the function of the human mind. Thus, the mind is assigned the convenient designation of black box. The black box

motif is a common one in science. It allows one to bypass an inexplicable entity and thereby proceed with a given theory.

The Skinnerian school of behavioral psychology bears the name of Burris F. Skinner. In the Skinnerian model of the mind as a black box, if one were to stimulate the "box" in an appropriate manner, one would witness a predictable response.

Related to this discussion is the philosophical dilemma of <u>solipsism</u> -- whether other minds or persons actually exist. The behavioral branch of psychology seems to answer in the negative. The concept of an <u>operational definition</u> in psychology is a case in point. Defining intelligence in terms of the score one receives on an I.Q. (Intelligence Quotient) test is to express intelligence in <u>operational</u> form. By doing so, the existence is denied of any facet of the mind not discernible to the administrator of the I.Q. test.

44. Friedrich Nietzche, <u>Beyond Good and Evil</u>, p. 45.

45. W.A. Sandholtz, "Nuclear Disarmament," <u>Chemical and Engineering News</u> 61(1983): 3.

46. <u>Der Zeitgeist</u> translates from the German as "spirit of the age".

47. Paul K. Feyerabend, <u>Science in a Free Society</u>, p. 74.

48. August Strindberg (1849-1912) was a playwright and novelist. It is noteworthy that he wrote this passage prior to even the First World War, much less the Holocaust. Strindberg's words were taken from Paul K. Feyerabend, <u>Against Method</u>. Compare the thought of Strindberg to that of David Landes in <u>Unbound Prometheus</u>, p. 554.

> In the meantime, the industrialization of the world proceeds for better or worse. This world, which has never before been ready to accept any of the universal faiths offered for its salvation, is apparently prepared to embrace the religion of science and technology without reservation.

49. The humanities were originally designated as such to delineate them from theology and religious study.

50. George C. Iggers, "The Idea of Progress: A Critical Reassessment," American Historical Review 71(1965): 1-17.

51. See Kren and Rappoport, Holocaust and the Crisis of Behavior, p. 139; and Feyerabend, Science, p. 27.

52. The terms science, scientific method, scientific mentality, and scientific rationality will be used almost interchangeably to prevent repetition.

53. Feyerabend, Science, p. 7.

54. Antoine De Saint-Exupery, The Little Prince, p. 18.

55. "Marketplace of ideas" was borrowed from a lecture delivered by Ms. Judy Krug at Gettysburg College in Gettysburg, Pennsylvania. Ms. Krug is director of the Office of Intellectual Freedom of the American Library Association in Chicago.

56. Cassandra was a Trojan princess of Greek legend who had learned the art of prophecy from Apollo, but was not believed.

57. Naturalism is the system of belief which contends that any attempt "to rearrange science or society with some explicit theories of rationality in mind would disturb the delicate balance of thought, emotion, imagination, ... and would create chaos, not perfection." Feyerabend, Science, p. 7.

The philosopher Thomas S. Kuhn objected to idealistic philosophies of science which wanted to reform society with the help of well-constructed blueprints.

58. For an example of writing diametrically opposed to my viewpoint, see Glenn Seaborg, "Science, Technology, and the Citizen," in The Place of Value in a World of Facts. eds. Arne Tiselius and Sam Nilsson, pp. 207-20. I am certain the Mr. Seaborg would consider my views anti-intellectual.

59. Emil L. Fackenheim, The Jewish Return into History, p. 5.

60. "Huston Smith has written: 'The moral is not 'less technology,' but 'more of other things': more checks on the concentration of power in politics, more attention to personal dimensions of life within society, more confidence in glimpses of reality sponsored by objectives other than science." Ian G. Barbour, Science and Security, p. 74.

Philosophers identify the deification of science as "scientism, a species of the intellectualist fallacy which finds science to be relevant to all human concerns, and all that is relevant." Abraham Kaplan, In Pursuit of Wisdom, p. 183.

61. Rubenstein, Age of Triage, pp. 16-17.

The Nazi objective was Gleichschaltung, "political unification and coordination", via the elimination of opposition. Compare Gleichschaltung with the German word, die Gleichartigkeit, which translates as "uniformity, homogeneity, and similarity".

It is not only totalitarian systems such as existed in Germany from 1933-45 which advocate and work towards social homogeneity. Democracies, in the name of universalism and equality-before-the-law, effect the same social leveling. See Pawlikowski, "Holocaust as Rational Event," p. 9; and Rubenstein, Age of Triage, p. 16. Paul K. Feyerabend notes that democratic principles as they are practiced today are incompatible with the undisturbed development, existence, and growth of special cultures such as Jewish and Afro-American. Feyerabend, Science, p. 78. The liberal notions that all men are brothers, and are essentially the same, function to reduce human particularity and identity. Consider the popular John Lennon song of the late 1970s entitled "Imagine" for an expression of such liberalism. Lennon's contention was that if there were no differences among people -- no religion, no possessions -- there would then be unity and peace.

People and groups which attempt to maintain a separate identity within Western democracies are subject to subtle pressures to relinquish their differences from the social norm. They are labeled obscurantist, though this is usually expressed in more overtly negative terms. In more repressive political contexts, such groups are actively and hostilely repressed, or exterminated. It is then science which provides the means for efficient extermination. Modern liberalism and humanism do not recognize the complementary value of a pluralism of traditions. I submit that human "sameness" does not equal quality living and peace.

63. Jacques Monod, "On Values in an Age of Science," in *The Place of Value in a World of Facts*, eds. Arne Tiselius and Sam Nilsson, p. 21.

64. *Phenotype*, a term from genetics, refers to outward or observable characteristics. Brown hair color is an example of phenotypic expression of innate genetic characteristics.

65. See Aryeh Carmell and Cyril Domb, eds., *Challenge*, p. 291.

66. Barbour, *Science and Secularity*, p. 70. *Eschatology* is the branch of theology concerned with the end of time and ultimate issues such as death, judgment, and heaven.

67. See Stanley Hauerwas, "Jews and Christians Among the Nations: The Social Significance of the Holocaust," *Cross Currents* 31(1981): 27, for the following:

> Far too often in order to sustain the premised universality of our convictions, they are transformed into general truths about 'being human' for which 'Christ' becomes a *handy* symbol. (underlining my own.)

68. Pawlikowski, *Challenge of Holocaust*, p. 11.

69. Jay W. Forrester, "Churches at the Transition Between Growth and World Equilibrium," in *Toward Global Equilibrium*, eds. Dennis L. Meadows and Donella H. Meadows, p. 346.

70. *Ibid.*, p. 350.

71. Feyerabend, *Science*, p. 80.

72. Liebe F. Cavalieri, "Genetic Engineering: Who Decides What?," *Baltimore Sun*, 16 January 1983, p. K3. Dr. Cavalieri is professor of biochemistry at Cornell University's Graduate School of Medical Sciences.

73. Joshua Lederberg, "Orthobiosis: The Perfection of Man," in The Place of Value in a World of Facts, eds. Arne Tiselius and Sam Nilsson, p. 54.

74. This motif was borrowed from Feyerabend, Science, p. 76.

75. Robert Jungk, "Altering the Direction of Technology," Cross Currents 20(1970): 135. Robert Jungk is founder of the Institut für Zukunftsfragen (Institute for Questions about the Future) in Vienna, Austria. He has taught at Technische Institut in Berlin.

76. Ibid. See Gordon Adams, The Politics of Defense Contracting , for a detailed look at how the future is being determined in the research and development departments of defense-related industries and in the Department of Defense.

77. Feyerabend, Science, p. 74.

78. Compare Franklin H. Littell, The Crucifixion of the Jews, p. 67:

> The real problem is that a single pattern of thinking has become normative in sociology as well as chemistry, in political science as well as engineering, in theology as well as nuclear physics. A prideful contempt for the human person, his present condition and his past experience ....

79. The degree to which the human component is eliminated is the measure of the reliability of scientific equipment and experimental procedures. Of course it is important to minimize human perceptual errors and biases from scientific endeavor, but to remove the reflexive, emotional element is to allow science and technology to be dehumanizing and ultimately lethal.

80. Bertrand Russell, Authority and the Individual.

81. Dr. Katz's thought used here was advanced at the Second Annual Conference on the Holocaust at Millersville University on 11 April 1983. The university is located in Millersville, Pennsylvania.

82. Kren and Rappoport, *Holocaust and the Crisis of Behavior*, p. 132. Such institutions include law, religion, and science.

CHAPTER VI

SPECIFIC PATHWAYS OF RESPONSE TO THE HOLOCAUST

The title of this book speaks of the imperative of response, the urgent need for change and redirection following the European Holocaust. This sense of urgency derives from understanding the Holocaust within the context of other human events of the twentieth century. Since the institutions and thought patterns regarded as beneficial to life also produced the Death Camps of Poland, fundamental re-evaluation of the trends of Western culture is in order. Those thought patterns which produced Auschwitz were not destroyed when the Germans dynamited that camp in advance of the Soviet army's drive west. In the course of contemplating changes in society, it is well to remember the admonition issued by Boris Pasternak in his work <u>Dr. Zhivago</u>: When life is put on the operating table to improve its ills, we need to be sure to keep it alive. Revolutionary, violent changes are not what this author advocates. Yet, more than minor adjustments are required in our thinking and perception of life after the Endlösung. A migration back to a less complicated worldview, wherein complex human interactions and problems are sidestepped by simplistic conceptions, will not be helpful.

Let us focus upon the scientific-rationalist trend which has dominated Western thought, response, and interpretation in the twentieth century. What this cultural trend has done with stunning success is encapsulate and submerge competing traditions, rendering such traditions relatively meaningless compared to the prominence of scientific mentality.(1) I submit that the merits of scientific rationality are not sufficient to warrant this tradition being the primary element in modern judgment and decision-making. Nor is the scientific trend sufficient as a means of bringing up children in state-supported public schools.(2) Agreement with the scientific-rationalist perspective should be the "result of examination and choice"(3) on the part of young people who are exposed to many alternative traditions in the course of their education. Theories of knowledge in addition to science need to be given access to the power of education. It is imperative that science not be presented as capable of explaining everything about life. What is particularly dangerous about the present role of scientific methodology in

121

education is that vast areas of human experience are considered relatively valueless because they cannot be subject to quantitative or computer analysis.(4) Because science does not have the capacity to adequately consider the emotional, spiritual, or mythic dimensions of human beings, these dimensions are assigned an importance value of almost zero in scientific motif.(5) In apparent attempt to provide value-free education for young people, we mistakenly believe scientific thinking will fulfill this goal. Yet, closer examination should reveal that far from being value-free, science is quite value-laden. Science may not comment directly on morality, for example, but by rendering religious perspectives unbelievable and deemphasizing human emotion, science is making value statements. Why is it that people cannot see that ostensibly non-committal, non-sectarian scientific posture about human beings does indeed constitute devaluation of life? The question becomes one of how to make science one tradition among many in the educational forum. A practical way to mitigate the power of scientific methodology and all its attendant problems would be to divorce science from state sponsorship(6) The power of religion was certainly lessened when it lost its secular arm, that is, the political state. Permit us to qualify what we mean by the separation of science and the state with respect to education: This suggestion is not to imply that scientific theories should not be presented in public schools. What is meant is that teachers need to present science per se, that is, biology, chemistry, etc., in a format such as: "Some people believe the theory of ..." or "This theory explains some things about ...". Moreover, the pervasiveness of scientific methodology in all subjects needs to be offset. Example: Even in English classes, one diagrams sentences to get to the basic elements and one dissects a novel to uncover symbolism, ironies, writing style, and various literary devices.(7) What is missing in both instances is an appreciation for the sentence or the novel as an entirety. The novel, for instance, remains fragmented as the result of analysis in the scientific spirit. The method espoused by modern education is how to use something rather than to have an understanding of that which one is using. Students learn how to use certain methods without comprehending what the specific methods are, who developed them, and how they were developed. Young people often do not know, and are not encouraged to care to know, any more than how to plug numbers into formulae or specific events into historical models and come out with an answer. American education in the past emphasized memorizing specific, concrete things such as the spelling of words, mathematical problems, historical chronologies, and important people. Memory took precedence over interpretation. The scientific approach in which analysis is paramount blurs and plays down any particularities in reality. Any notion of wholeness and completeness about reality is submerged. Let us consider how an English teacher might use a poem about a person to counterbalance scientific-rational thinking. The teacher would need to emphasize that the students could learn about and know about people from that poem in ways no less valid than the results of psychological and biological measurement. Likewise, an essay about trees which speaks in terms of beauty, form, and contour helps us to know about trees in a manner which complements scientific knowledge. Why should, "a graceful, flowering dogwood tree", tell us less than "a Cornus florida specimen five meters high"? The following depiction of one possible theory of knowledge attempts to demonstrate the complementary nature of different traditions. This author asserts that the scientific tradition does not totally subsume other traditions such as religious and philosophical, but merely overlaps with them at certain points. Additional scientific knowledge and new scientific theories, therefore, are not to be viewed as a linear progression towards overarching Truth. Rather, new knowledge simply presents us with more information for the development of our consciousness.(8) (See Figure 1)

Another example of the pervasiveness of scientific mentality throughout education comes from the discipline of psychology. This study of people, their minds, personalities, and behaviors, ignores the dimensions about a person which cannot be measured. I.Q. does not really tell us much more about the human mind than a particular person's ability to correctly respond to a group of problems limited in scope of examination.(9)

Modern education conducted in the rationalist Zeitgeist corrupts young children's perceptions of reality by essentially disallowing thought and language not reflective of the results of sensory data. That which does not conform with what we sense directly(10) or with the aid of instruments is considered inaccurate, and thus unacceptable. An emphasis on the philosophic perspective in public schools and colleges would provide a countervailing force to the scientific viewpoint. Philosophy does not stand in awe of sensory analysis, but rigorously questions the accuracy and reality of the knowledge derived from the senses.

Figure 1

A Different Theory of Knowledge

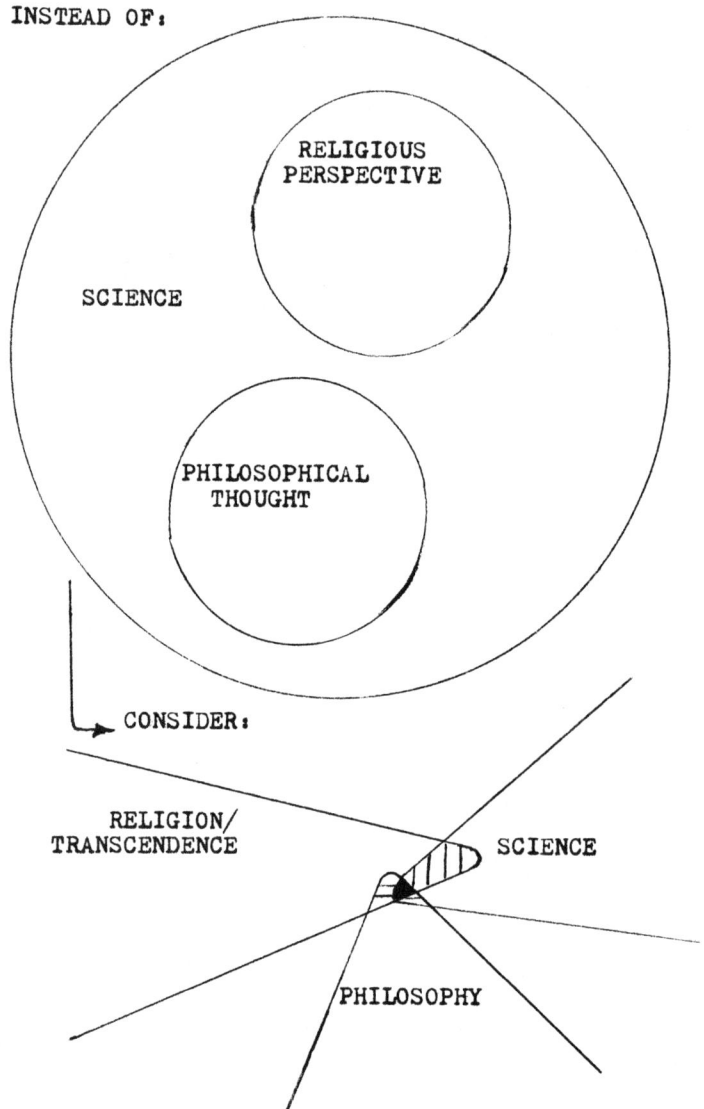

Drawing by Robert S. Frey

Philosophy cultivates the art of <u>thinking</u> over and above <u>analysis</u>. Pure thought is a vital complement to quantitative consideration of reality. Another complementary perspective is the spiritual-transcendent tradition. I recognize the repugnance this recommendation will cause in the American Jewish community and among the membership of the American Civil Liberties Union, for example. The separation of church and state relations is firmly entrenched in intellectual, liberal circles in America. I am aware that the public schools, simply by virtue of a premium on time, cannot hope to present the many religious traditions in a vital, living context. My point in raising this issue is not to advocate a neutered, non-sectarian civil religion(11) being presented as transcendent perspective in our state-supported educational institutions. I do think that it is necessary for schools at the very least to make students aware that a religious interpretation of reality can help us <u>know</u> certain things about human beings and life in general.(12) The scientific perspective does not help students deal with such questions as "Why do people exist?" and "What is the purpose of life?" The transcendent dimension in human experience can be given legitimacy if it is not totally discounted or ignored by the educational process.(13) An example of the need for the transcendent tradition of interpreting reality may prove helpful at this point. Some scholars have concluded that the Holocaust demonstrates that morality derives only from the efforts and choices of the individual human will.(14) If the Holocaust were discussed in-depth in schools, (which it is not to any great degree) this viewpoint could be advanced with no risk of litigation on the basis of abridgment of First Amendment rights. Yet what does this viewpoint imply? Following therefrom, nothing in this world, it would seem, would be stable. What will cause man to want to, that is, <u>will</u> himself to be moral? I submit that consideration of a spiritual dimension in other people, and an overarching spiritual dimension in the world, will do so.(15) It should be apparent that students subject to a scientific-rationalist education will <u>not</u> realize the need for the behavioral restraints of the spiritual dimension. Such behavioral restraints deriving from a recognition of transcendent values will be what will help mankind become secure from annihilation. Education in America must come to recognize the value of a pluralism of ideas and methodologies. Having people raised with one ideology sets the stage for manipulation by governments and for prejudice against groups that do not conform to that ideology.

The scientific-rationalist spirit is not indigenous only to modern education, but actually is the matrix for the entire era. As in the case of education, the religious perspective could also provide vital counterbalance in the public domain. The social ethicist John T. Pawlikowski has recognized this need when he asked, "How do we establish the formal and informal channels whereby religion can exercise a constructive influence on public morality without imposing a particular moral perspective on the body politic?"(16) "A constructive influence on public morality" takes on significant importation given this author's thesis that the Holocaust was the result of thought patterns and institutions with no moral direction."(17) Separation of church and state must not be so strictly interpreted contitutionally so as to allow no space of legitimacy for religious viewpoint in public policy formation and decision-making. Bureaucracy that is inundated with decision-makers, who have no sense of the Transcendent with its concomitant moral perimeters, or, who are capable of separating decisions from their sense of values, is especially ominous if the religious perspective has no access to political judgments. Irving Greenberg speaks of a "holy secularism", a term suggesting the synthesis of transcendental values and scientific-rationality; a vision of transcendence rooted in the world. From these statements, one might conclude that if only the Western world would turn back to religion, another Holocaust could not occur. In addition, if religious vision had been paramount in 1933, the Holocaust would not have happened. It can be argued, however, that much has been perpetrated in the name of religion to the detriment of mankind. "How about the I.R.A.(18) and its terrorism, ... or the pogroms of Russian Orthodox peasants against Jews in Kishinev, Russia, in 1912, or Protestant assaults on Catholics in Baltimore during the Know-Nothingism of the 1840s...?"(19) We could also include the Crusades and Thomas de Torquemada's politico-religious Inquisition in Spain. Yet let us also consider: "Were the barbarities perpetrated at Auschwitz or the fire-bombing of Dresden prompted by religious convictions? Were the twenty million Nationalist Chinese slaughtered by Mao, or the civilian population of My Lai murdered by American soldiers, the victims of a theological crusade?"(20) To this list we might add Hiroshima, the Japanese medical experiments on prisoners-of-war in Manchuria, and the murder of South American Indian populations at the hands of government troops. If we have difficulty accepting the premise that a reinvestment in things spiritual is called for in the wake of HaShoah, we must also ask what will serve to control human behavior if not G-d? Mankind has not lost its real need for mythic expression. Rationalism, however, will argue that ritualistic "mumbo-jumbo" is meaningless. Yet the Nazi elite recognized the power of ritual behavior and symbols. "They were quite aware that symbols bind people in ways that ideas alone cannot. They understood that acts of celebration strengthen resolve in ways that mere discussion cannot."(21) In a similar manner, religious ritual can accomplish much more in the way of building a consensus of feeling(22) among a diverse population such as exists in America than rational discussion can ever hope to do. The religious perspective, if provided the avenue of expression, could complement the rational tone of modern political judgment with a concern and a response based upon human feelings and empathy. The reflexive element in human beings is recognized by religion as having value. Such scholars as Richard L. Rubenstein, George M. Kren, Leon Rappoport, and Henry Feingold(23) have concluded that the modern political state is the most powerful entity on the face of the earth, bar none. As such, it could be argued that the contemporary nation-state could engulf, nullify the efforts of, or ally itself with organized religion, thereby rendering religion functionally valueless. Yet there exists no other institution in Western culture which could provide counterbalance to governmental positions, and do so from a foundation of transcendent morality. Any new and expanded role of religion in public policy decisions, however, cannot be premised upon a simple return to Biblicism.(24) Religious fanaticism is not an adequate or desirable response to the scientific-rationalist milieu. Indeed, religion as it has been experienced by most people in Western societies will not bind man's behavior in moral channels. Religious perspective based primarily upon curbing human emotions and appetites will be insufficient because scientific mentality has the same effect. The spiritual perspective will have to expand and reinterpret its role to include the affirmation of human emotion in an age of reason which has Auschwitz as a monument to its rational thought. The questioning of authority also requires the moral sanction of the religious community in America. Governments benefit from the separation of religion and state because the religious perspective is denied access to the political decision-making process.

Related to the need for recognition of a plurality of perspectives on reality is the need in Western society for affirming the differences among peoples to be good. Instead of the modern tendency to submerge human identity in the seemingly admirable construct of universal brotherhood, let us affirm particular points that differ from group to group as being beneficial. Universalism and cultural homogeneity are not the roads to peace; they are the tracks to total domination of a culture by a government. Strengthening group identity is not too high a price to pay for creative diversity, cultural health, and human political freedom. If modern governments allied with science are not to be the sole determinants of our future, Robert Jungk, a European futurist, believes that we must develop new "'future creating' institutions" to counterbalance governmental RAND Corporations,(25) that is, think tanks and research and development institutions. Dr. Jungk maintains that we must "invent" futures which are human-oriented because the tomorrows envisioned by government and industry were envisioned with "economic, political and military power in mind."(26) It is certainly evident in American society that the best minds in the country are not engaged in determining and imagining how to help people live together better and more happily.(27) We have the capability to ease so many of the problems that suffocate and thwart quality living. There could be so many people engaged in exploring alternative modes of living and different ways of conducting business, administering law, educating young people, designing communities, etc. Arthur I. Waskow argues that "one of the major tasks of intellectuals today is to assist the many publics in their countries to imagine the future, so that the future may be created more democratically than now looks likely. ...One of the most powerful ways of achieving social change is to imagine in vivid detail a desirable and achievable future, and then build a part of that future in the present - rather than merely pleading that it be built."(28) Waskow continues, "Decisions on research and development of weapons systems made today will affect what the world looks like twenty years from now. They will affect, for example, whether it is even possible to achieve a disarmed world then."(29) The governmental policies of the Nazis may well approach this motif of Arthur Waskow's. Let us consider that the Nazi elite imagined a Judenrein(30) Europe in the early 1930s. They envisioned a possible future, and set legal and political mechanisms in motion to achieve their objective. By the time people became cognizant of the Nazi "future", alternatives had not been developed and avenues of moving in another direction had been closed by legal means. "Anger and revulsion"(31) in 1942 would have meant little against a Nazi vision which had already assumed the proportion of a national system and the legitimacy of being a rational direction vis-a-vis the Jewish Question. Precisely because governments are engaged in creating the future argues strongly for private, civilian institutions pursuing alternatives to governmental vision.

An example of specific governmental action that should be taken given the reality of the concentration camp universe of Europe is ratification of the Genocide Pact.(32) Passed by the General Assembly of the United Nations, this treaty was introduced for ratification to the United States Senate in June 1949 by President Harry S. Truman. The Genocide Resolution declares "genocide a crime under international law",(33) and originated from worldwide reaction to the Nazi extermination program. To date, nearly eighty-five countries have formally ratified the Genocide Treaty. The United States, however, has not done so. "Specifically, the genocide treaty became trapped in the civil rights - U.S. vs. states - struggles that dominated the politics of the 1950s and early 1960s. It became a controversial example of internationalism and of the possibilities that its sanctions against human-rights abuses could be applied internally to incidents in this country, especially during the bloody civil rights confrontations that occurred in the Deep South."(34) By ratifying the Genocide Pact, the United States would be issuing a clear statement of its stance towards Nazi "war criminals" and all perpetrators of genocide. Genocide is the deliberate attempt to destroy a people in terms of physical extermination and/or eradication of its particular culture and way of life. By way of challenge to the necessity of ratification, let us consider the following. One might well argue that the Western governments of the 1930s and 1940s had officially adopted many humanitarian principles; yet, for whatever reasons, chose to severely limit the practical applications of such principles with respect to European Jews. In this context, what good would one more official statement affirming respect for humanity mean? This case can be extended beyond governments to religious institutions and social organizations. These organizations, all of which espoused an ostensibly humanitarian outlook, also did not alleviate Jewish suffering in any concerted, planned manner. Therefore, would official Church statements on human dignity, for example, delivered in 1985, have any functional validity? Would such statements actually be reified when conditions demanded concrete action? I do believe that however limited the impact is of official Church statements or the Genocide Pact, they should be advanced, ratified, and affirmed. Such affirmations of the value of human beings at least provide an ideal to advance towards and for which to sacrifice security, time, and effort. Official government statements, religious doctrines, and organizational charters should not, however, confuse and dupe us into accepting certain illusions about contemporary Western culture that were made manifest by the Holocaust. <u>The Holocaust provides cogent evidence against the existence of an humanitarian framework to human culture.</u>(35) Auschwitz argues that people do not truly care for other people. There is no special sanctity to life, no special realm of awe and respect reserved for human beings in <u>any functional sense of the words sanctity, awe, and respect</u>. HaShoah exposes in graphic relief the fallacy of the notion that <u>civilized</u> people do not engage in certain behaviors. Civilization and barbarous actions are not mutually exclusive. Another modern illusion, that real moral progress is occurring at a societal level, must also be foresworn until hard evidence suggests otherwise. The tragedy of these illusions in which society has so heavily invested is that whole peoples have staked their very existence upon them. The Jews of Europe in the late 1930s and early 1940s kept looking for humanitarian intervention from the West -- it never came. Many Jews survived, or died, specifically in an attempt to provide the world with information it too often chooses to dismiss. Dismissal of Jewish testimony follows from a general reluctance to let go of the cultural mirages by which we maintain tenuous stability and hope in the modern era. Why can't we face life without such fictions, admit what actually is the case, and proceed to deal with things in the light of that reality.(36) In need of close examination is the collective moral posture of our institutions which operate with pre-Holocaust mentality, continuing to speak of world conscience and moral progress as fact. To knowingly dispense false hope and security after the Holocaust is detestable from a moral perspective. Therefore, in light of HaShoah, sharp delineation must be established between human ideals, social reality, and illusions. A case in point is that of human rights. Richard L. Rubenstein has argued that human rights have meaning only when the group that claims them has the power to sustain the claim.(37) Inalienable rights, that is, liberties which are guaranteed solely by virtue of the fact of one being human, are thus illusions. Rights are quickly revoked or limited in cases of national emergency or when they infringe upon national security. The 112,000 Japanese-Americans interned in camps during World War II provide an example of such abridgment of rights in the name of national security. Seventy thousand of those people were United States citizens by birth.(38) Jews who were stripped of German citizenship and then denied citizenship from any other country were stateless, powerless, and without civil rights. No international codex of inalienable rights picked up where the privileges of citizenship left off. Nevertheless, First Amendment constitutional "rights" must be made as strong as possible in these United States. They remain the sole legal protection of human dignity and quality living in America.

Many of the ideas discussed to this point have involved education and the installation of value-making capacity in young people. To pursue this general direction further, I submit that some form of youth national service(39) would be extremely beneficial in this post-Holocaust era. Young people in the final two years of high school, at the idealistic ages of sixteen and seventeen, would serve in a mandatory social service capacity. If this program were integrated directly into one's conception of being a teenager and was required for high school graduation, it might become less of a burden. Such a program would answer the often heard complaint that formal education is not reflective of, or involved in, the real world. Students might be assigned work with the physically and mentally handicapped, migrant farmworkers, and juvenile offenders to list just several examples. The development of a workable model community would be another possibility worth pursuing. An intrastate student exchange system, if inaugurated, would allow young people to experience a different living environment and diverse traditions and perspectives. The program could be instituted during the summers prior to the junior and senior years of high school rather than during the academic year itself. By not only studying about, but by actually living amidst people with different backgrounds, values, and ideas, a young person might come to realize that many dimensions and outlooks are present in the human community. The timing of the national service in terms of the student's age would allow the heart-felt idealism of youth a meaningful outlet. Young people may come away from their social service experience with a greater appreciation of social problems, human differences, and the mechanics of public decision-making. As such, they may work more constructively to change the problems they see.

The Holocaust demands a reorientation of Western culture away from a monolithic, value-free scientific mentality. Social health requires the cultivation of non-scientific alternative traditions which are provided access to important decision-making. Nuclear weapons and death factories were not engineered in response to intangible fears and violence-prone emotions.(40) They are the products of rational decisions made in response to systemically-defined problems. Counterbalance is imperative.

NOTES

CHAPTER VI

SPECIFIC PATHWAYS OF RESPONSE TO THE HOLOCAUST

1. The French sociologist Michael Crozier has warned, "'Beware of the temptation -- difficult to resist -- of the arrogance of rationality'"; it is, "'a kind of folly' to assume that 'a rational view of the world based on the inevitability of scientific progress can cope with a fragmented, culturally diverse society ....'" Cited in Glenn Seaborg, "Science, Technology, and the Citizen," in The Place of Value in a World of Facts, eds. Arne Tiselius and Sam Nilsson, p. 212. Michael Crozier is founder and director of the Centre de Sociologie des Organisations in Paris and is Senior Research Director of the Centre Nationale de la Recherche Scientifique. He has taught at Harvard, Berkeley, and Chicago.

2. Paul K. Feyerabend, Against Method, p. 217.

3. Ibid.

4. Time magazine "reports MIT computer professor Joseph Weizenbaum worrying that 'the whole world is made to seem computable. This generates a kind of tunnel vision, where the only problems that seem legitimate are problems that can be put on a computer'." Cited by Bernard Fryshman, "Computer Teaching in the Yeshiva: Processing the Data, Programming the Risks," Jewish Observer 16(1983): 15. Dr. Fryshman is associate professor of physics at the New York Institute of Technology.

5. Paul K. Feyerabend provides a specific example of science's claim to be the only legitimate means to acquire and express knowledge. Consider oracles and rain dances. These phenomena are interpreted by anthropologists as expressions of the needs of members of a society, as functioning as social glue, as revealing basic structures of thought. Anthropologists may even admit that oracles and rain dances lead to increased awareness of the relations between man and man, and man and nature. However, these phenomena are not interpreted as means of gaining knowledge or knowing about rain or spirit-related dimensions. Paul K. Feyerabend, Science in a Free Society, p. 77.

6. Feyerabend, Against Method, p. 216.

7. An example of a literary device is alliteration -- the use of repetitive, similar sounds in a given sentence.

8. Feyerabend, Against Method, p. 160.

9. I.Q. test results can also be compared over a large number of people in the effort to perceive patterns in age groups, population segments, ethnic groups, and geographical regions.

10. "Sense directly" refers to what one perceives with his physical sense organs.

11. For a definitive treatment of the concept of civil religion, see Robert N. Bellah, "Civil Religion in America," Daedalus 96(1967): 1-21.

12. Of note on the topic of schools and religion is the Jerusalem Academy. Founded in 1970, it was the first Jewish school which specialized in educating students with limited Jewish background in Torah-learning. Students are eventually enabled to relate the teachings contained in the Torah to modern-day problems. Relating religious sources to contemporary dilemmas and concerns is what is vital today.

13. From the writer Edwin A. Abbott comes this interesting call to appreciate more than one interpretation of reality:

> ... it is as natural for us Flatlanders to lock up a Square for preaching the Third dimension, as it is for you Spacelanders to lock up a Cube for preaching the Fourth. Alas, how strong a family likeness runs through blind and persecuting humanity in all Dimensions!

Edwin A. Abbott, Flatland, preface.

> Compare Feyerabend, Science, p. 79: Must we not demand that ideas and procedures that give substance to the lives of people be made full members of a free society no matter what other traditions think about them?

14. George M. Kren and Leon Rappoport, The Holocaust and the Crisis of Human Behavior, p. 142: "Insofar as morality exists, even as a concept, it does so as an act of the all-too-fallible human will."

15. "Seeing" the other person as being more than the synthesis of mind and body is a step in the right direction. The Orthodox Jewish view of personhood speaks to this primary dilemma of the Holocaust. In the Jewish perspective, each person is seen to be an entire world in and of himself. If people were to act on more than one dimension and view others as being a myriad of dimensions, this may go far to deflect the tendency towards dehumanization which is present in our society.

16. John T. Pawlikowski, "The Holocaust: Its Implications for the Church and Society Problematic," Encounter 42 (1981): 148.

17. The transcendent dimension is vital in light of the observation "that the multidimensionality of human existence has virtually shrunk to the level of a single dimension -- that of technology and economy. ...'Western society requires the individual to choose without values (repression of the normative); to work without meaning (repression of the spiritual); to integrate without community (repression of the communal dimension). One could add: to think without feeling (repression of the affective) and to live without faith, hope, myth, utopia (repression of the transcendental dimension).'" Pawlikowski, "The Holocaust," p. 145.

See also John T. Pawlikowski, "Church-State Relations: A Contemporary Catholic Perspective," mimeographed; and Irving Greenberg, "Judaism and Christianity after the Holocaust," Journal of Ecumenical Studies 12(1975): 536 -- "Secular authority unchecked becomes absolute. After the Holocaust it is all the more urgent to resist this absolutization of the secular." Several other noted scholars recognize the need for the religious perspective to be involved in public affairs. These include Franklin H. Littell, John C. Raines, Manfred Vogel, Richard Neuhaus, Sydney Mead, and Clyde Manschreck. John C. Raines, a Christian, is professor of religion at Temple University. Manfred Vogel (Jewish) is professor of religion at Northwestern University. Richard Neuhaus is a pastor and social commentator. He also serves as Consulting Editor of Worldview magazine. Sydney Mead is an historian at

Yale University, and Clyde Manschreck is a Church historian retired from Chicago Theological Seminary.

For an example of the practical expression of the religious viewpoint in the public domain, see D.J.R. Bruckner, "Chicago's Activist Cardinal," New York Times Magazine, 1 May 1983, pp. 42-92. This article describes the work of Cardinal Joseph Bernardin in his fight to confront nuclear strategy with religious morality.

18. I.R.A. refers to the Irish Republican Army.

19. Mayer Schiller, The Road Back, p. 68.

20. Ibid.

21. Pawlikowski, "Church-State Relations," p. 21.

22. A religious consensus is something which Richard L. Rubenstein calls for in The Age of Triage.

23. "They (American Jewry) did not understand that the nation-state was dangerously out of control, that all moral and ethical restraints had vanished and only countervailing power held it in check." Henry L. Feingold, "Who Shall Bear Guilt for the Holocaust: The Human Dilemma," American Jewish History 68(1979): 281.

24. This thought was borrowed from a lecture given by John T. Pawlikowski at the Bernhard E. Olson Scholars' Conference on the Holocaust held in New York in March, 1983.

25. Robert Jungk, "Altering the Direction of Technology," Cross Currents 20(1970): 135. The RAND Corporation, according to Arthur I. Waskow, began with concern for the future of military strategy and branched into the area of general interest in the future of official American policy. Oriented to the group of people that runs the United States government, the RAND Corporation is based on the notion that planning need not, ought not, and could not be, in any sense, the property of the American people. Arthur I. Waskow, "Looking Forward: 1999," in Mankind 2000, eds. Robert Jungk and Johan Galtung, p. 78.

Consider the thought of Eliezer Ben-David with regard to public involvement in scientific activity and the military. "In the Nuclear Age, mankind cannot afford to allow science to proceed unregulated and without moral guidance. The stakes are too high and the danger is too great. Just as the Dor Hahaflaga had to end in a cataclysm because of their misuse of great knowledge, so our age must seek to carefully moniter [sic] the activities of scientists to ensure that their knowledge will be used only for mankind. Just as the military needs civilian supervision, so must those who deal purely in science have an objective and morally watchful eye constantly over them." Eliezer Ben-David, Out of the Iron Furnace, p. 52. Dor Hahaflaga refers to the people who were involved in building the tower of Babel.

26. Jungk, "Altering Technology," p. 135.

27. It is also apparent that national budgets are not designed around pressing community and familial needs such as day care, housing, education, medical care, job training, and recreational facilities.

28. Waskow, "Looking Forward," p. 78. At the time of the publication of his section of Mankind 2000, Waskow was with the Institute for Policy Studies in Washington, D.C.

29. Ibid., p. 79. See also, Gordon Adams, The Politics of Defense Contracting. With defense industries pressuring the Federal government for funding to develop new weapons systems so that defense-related jobs are secure and the industrial structure in given geographic areas remains intact, disarmament and weapons de-escalation appear remote.

30. Judenrein translates from the German as "free of Jews".

31. Waskow, "Looking Forward," p. 79.

32. Haynes Johnson, "Reagan's Eloquence Can't Mask Failure to Push Genocide Pact," Washington Post, 17 April 1983, p. A3.

33. Ibid.

34. Ibid., p. A3.

35. As Henry L. Feingold notes, "The indictment of the witnesses is based on the old assumption that there exists such a spirit of civilization, a sense of humanitarian concern in the world, which could have

been mobilized to save Jewish lives during the Holocaust. It indicts the Roosevelt administration, the Vatican, the British government and all other witnessing nations and agencies for not acting, for not caring, and it reserves a special indignation for American Jewry's failure to mobilize a spirit which did not in fact exist." (underlining my own) Feingold, "Who Shall Bear Guilt," pp. 281-282.

36. In addition to dismissing cultural illusions, it would behoove schools not to hide, suppress, or skew information imparted to young people regarding governmental and economic systems. Capitalism, socialism, communism, democracy, and monarchy, for example, need balanced presentation. Western biases should not be manifested in the learning process. The only way to explore current thought patterns, ideas, and institutions is to have access to accurate information about such options.

37. Richard L. Rubenstein, The Cunning of History, pp. 89, 91.

A state might allow dissent up to a point, but no state will knowingly permit any internal or external group or individual to usurp its power. Every organization has but one code of ethics -- survive at any cost. In effect, keep those in power there in power. Modern governments have the means to effect that end.

38. Isidore Starr, "Human Rights in Time of Crisis," in Human Rights in the United States, pp. 81-98. Specific Supreme Court cases upholding the military evacuation of the Japanese-Americans included Hirabayashi v. United States (1943) and Korematsu v. United States (1944). The Korematsu case may be reopened in the near future. For an update of the efforts of Japanese-Americans to receive just compensation for internment and loss of property and income, see "38 Japanese-Americans to Get Compensation," New York Times, 22 May 1983, p. 18.

See also, Robert Justin Goldstein, "The FBI's Forty Year Plot," Nation 227(1978): 10-15, which concerns the internment of Japanese-Americans.

39. Young people in Israel, both men and women, have mandatory military service following the completion of high school. Men serve three years; women

serve two years. If Orthodox religious reasons prohibit military service, national social service is done instead.

40. My argument here is contra-Sandholtz, who contends that nuclear hardware and stockpiles "are merely the tangible evidences of the intangible fears and emotions which motivate violence." W.A. Sandholtz, "Nuclear Disarmament," *Chemical and Engineering News* 61(1983): 3. Evidently W.A. Sandholtz believes that without runaway emotion on the part of society, science would never have produced such things as nuclear weapons.

CHAPTER VII

THE HOLOCAUST RECONSIDERED

There remain several points which deserve discussion in this work. Foremost among these is a fundamental platform espoused by the eloquent writer, professor, and Holocaust survivor -- Elie Wiesel. Wiesel ardently asserts that no one except the survivor can ever know about the reality of the Holocaust. Auschwitz remains impenetrable to all who approach its gates from the outside seeking to learn of its mystery and rational terror.(1) According to this line of thought, no one other than the survivor can legitimately comment upon and study the Holocaust, much less comprehend it or suggest interpretations. With a single stroke, Wiesel's argument neutralizes the many important contributions to Holocaust understanding offered by non-survivors. When extrapolated, Wiesel's notion leads to the conclusion that once all the survivors have died, nothing will be added to the collection of knowledge and interpretation of HaShoah. This author fails to perceive the benefit of such privatization of the Holocaust event. The Holocaust is a dilemma of <u>human</u> <u>proportion</u>. To purposefully limit the understanding of l'holocauste to a select group of individuals needlessly precludes many human sources of insight. There is no advantage to be gained if the Western world continues to view the Holocaust as only a Jewish problem. Such perspective leads to the homogenization of the Endlösung into other human suffering. I believe that the <u>Jewish</u> focus of HaShoah can be maintained and affirmed without excluding the event from <u>public</u> consideration and understanding. In fairness, I can empathize with Wiesel's feeling that no one who did not directly encounter the monumental evil of the concentration camp universe could begin to understand the Holocaust. Yet <u>HaShoah</u> <u>cannot</u> <u>be</u> <u>perceived</u> <u>only</u> <u>in</u> <u>terms</u> <u>of</u> <u>human</u> <u>suffering</u>. The synthesis of base and benign forces which produced the Nazi extermination program can in fact be examined and interpreted without direct experience of that program's lethal impact. Particular human suffering does not encompass the reality of the Final Solution. Patterns of thought and institutions involved in producing the Endlosung need critical evaluation by many more people than those who were directly trapped in the Nazi onslaught against European Jewry. As with the victims, the human proportions of HaShoah must also be recognized when considering the perpetrators of this event.

The Holocaust should not and cannot be understood only in terms of the Nazis. The German nation and German people are not alone in the capacity to commit mass murder. The Endlösung must not be used to flagellate contemporary Germans into feeling guilty. Instead, what needs to be recognized is that in the wake of the Holocaust, the majority of Western culture stands indicted as morally bankrupt. The Nazi elite simply harnessed what was already extant -- the reflex of anti-Semitism, scientific-rational thinking, and bureaucracy to name only a few. When the primary constructs of one's way of life are called into serious question, positive, fundamental change is not usually the initial response. The prospect of widespread, deep-seated re-evaluation and redirection is dismissed as too involved, too time-consuming, and perhaps unnecessary. Because overarching change and response to HaShoah require commitment, vision, imagination, and concern, there is little probability it will occur soon. Yet the forces by which Auschwitz was forged persist, whether we choose to recognize them or not. Many of those trends not only persist, but are actively nurtured.

Because the Holocaust is an event of universal human dimension and import does not mean that the concept of holocaust can be appropriated at will to describe other human dilemmas. Already the term holocaust is applied to abortion, the nuclear reactor accident at Three Mile Island in Middletown, Pennsylvania (March, 1979), and the specter of nuclear war. I submit that Holocaust should remain as the distinctive term by which the destruction of European Jewry is known. Holocaust should continue to provide particularity for the Jewish suffering.

It is discouraging to hear learned, informed individuals comment that everything which can be said about the Holocaust has been presented already. According to such thinking, since the Holocaust has been sufficiently "explained" in terms of conventional wisdom, it should be let alone. That the Holocaust might provide part of an on-going perspective by which cultural trends and patterns of thought could be evaluated is apparently not considered. It is not surprising, however, that we want to bury the Holocaust beneath historic time, given our propensity to conceal and forget the unpleasant and ugly. Witness our treatment of death, physical impairment, aging, and mental retardation for a glimpse of this tendency. The meaning and importance of the Holocaust for contemporary life remain poorly demonstrated. Explanations of this event abound; there is no excess, however, of overarching interpretation and response.

NOTES

CHAPTER VII

THE HOLOCAUST RECONSIDERED

1. Elie Wiesel, "Foreword," in <u>A Christian Response to the Holocaust</u>, Harry James Cargas, p. iii; and in Elie Wiesel, "Art and Culture after the Holocaust," in <u>Auschwitz: Beginning of a New Era?</u>, ed. Eva Marie Fleischner, p. 405.

BIBLIOGRAPHY

The majority of sources cited herein approach the Holocaust from a theological, historical, and/or sociological perspective. This is because HaShoah has been treated overwhelmingly according to these modes of inquiry and expression. Personal narratives and eyewitness accounts also contribute heavily to the corpus of Holocaust literature. To date, there are relatively few works which approach the Holocaust from several directions simultaneously.

Abbott, Edwin A. Flatland. A Romance of Many Dimensions. 6th ed., rev. New York: Dover, 1952.

Adams, Gordon. The Politics of Defense Contracting: The Iron Triangle. New Brunswick, N.J.: Transaction Bks, 1982.

Anotoli, A. Babi Yar: A Document in the Form of a Novel. Translated by David Floyd. New York: FS&G, 1970. The author's full name is Anatoli Vasilevich Kuznetsov.

Arens, Richard. "Dr. Mengele's New Victims," New York Times, 28 March 1979, p. A24.

Dr. Richard Arens is the brother of Israel Defense Minister Moshe Arens.

------., ed. Genocide in Paraguay. Philadelphia: Temple U Pr, 1976.

Arlen, Michael J. Passage to Ararat. New York: FS&G, 1975.

Aronsfeld, C. C. "The Extermination of the Jews Was No 'War Crime'," Contemporary Review 231(1977): 145-48.

Asheri, Michael. Living Jewish: The Lore and Law of Being a Practicing Jew. 2d ed. New York: Everest Hse, 1980.

Barbour, Ian G. Science and Secularity: The Ethics of Technology. New York: Har-Row, 1970.

Baron, Salo W. "Changing Patterns of Antisemitism: A Survey." Jewish Social Studies 38(1976): 5-38.

Barrett, William. *Irrational Man: A Study in Existential Philosophy*. Garden City, N.Y.: Doubleday, 1958.

Baum, Gregory G. *Man Becoming: God in Secular Experience*. New York: Herder, 1970.

Baum, Ranier C. *The Holocaust and the German Elite: Genocide and National Suicide in Germany, 1871-1945*. Totowa, N.J.: Rowman, 1981.

Bellah, Robert N. "Civil Religion in America." *Daedalus* 96(1967): 1-21.

Ben-David, Eliezer. *Out of the Iron Furnace: The Jewish Redemption from Ancient Egypt and the Delivery from Spiritual Bondage*. Translated by Yaakov Feitman. New York: Shengold, 1975.

Berkovits, Eliezer. *Faith after the Holocaust*. New York: Ktav, 1973.

Berman, Morris. *The Reenchantment of the World*. Ithaca: Cornell U Pr, 1981.

Blum, Howard. *Wanted!: The Search for Nazis in Americas*. Greenwich, Conn.: Fawcett, 1977.

Bokser, Ben Zion. *Judaism and the Christian Predicament*. New York: Knopf, 1967.

Bonhoeffer, Dietrich. *Prisoner of God: Letters and Papers from Prison*. Translated by Reginald H. Fuller. New York: Macmillan, 1953.

Borkin, Joseph. *The Crime and Punishment of I. G. Farben*. New York: Free Pr, 1978.

Borowitz, Eugene B. "Liberal Jews in Search of an 'Absolute'." *Cross Currents* 29(1979): 9-14.

Boulding, Kenneth E., and Clark, Henry. *Human Values on the Spaceship Earth*. New York: National Council of the Churches of Christ in the U.S.A., 1966.

Braham, Randolph L., ed. *Perspectives on the Holocaust*. Boston: Kluwer-Nijhoff, 1983.

Part of the Holocaust Studies Series published in association with the Jack P. Eisner Institute for Holocaust Studies.

Brown, Robert McAfee. "The Holocaust: The Crisis of Indifference." Conservative Judaism 31(1976-77): 16-20.

------. The Pseudonyms of God. Philadelphia: Westminster, 1972.

Bruckner, D.J.R. "Chicago's Activist Cardinal," New York Times Magazine, 1 May 1983, pp. 42-92.

Mr. Bruckner is an editor in the Sunday Book Review section of the Times.

Brugioni, Dino A., and Poirier, Robert G. The Holocaust Revisited: A Retrospective Analysis of the Auschwitz-Birkenau Extermination Complex. Washington, D.C.: Central Intelligence Agency, 1979. Document Number ST-79-10001.

This work contains aerial photographs of Auschwitz-Birkenau in operation.

Buchanan, George Wesley. "Jewish and Christian Relationships." Religion in Life 40(1971): 273-79.

Buser, Michael B. Auschwitz as Revelation. Washington, D.C.: Georgetown U Pr, 1974.

Butz, Arthur R. The Hoax of the Twentieth Century. Torrance, Calif.: Inst Hist Rev, 1979.

Dr. Butz is now an associate professor of Electrical Engineering and Computer Sciences at Northwestern University in Evanston, Illinois. He is a graduate of MIT and the University of Minnesota. His book is an example of pseudo-revisionist history. Butz's arguments will not evaporate simply because he is addressing a topic outside his field of expertise.

Cain, Seymour. "The Questions and Answers after Auschwitz." Judaism 20(1971): 263-78.

Cargas, Harry James. A Christian Response to the Holocaust. Denver: Stonehenge, 1981.

The book has a foreword by Elie Wiesel. One of the primary contributions of Dr. Cargas' work herein is the collection of Holocaust photographs and commentary.

------. The Holocaust: An Annotated Bibliography. Haverford, Pa.: Cath Lib Assn, 1977.

------. "A Post-Auschwitz Catholic." Christian Century 95(1978): 1063-4.

------. "Time to Excommunicate Adolf Hitler, R.C." National Catholic Reporter 16(1980): 13.

------. "World Literature and the Holocaust." Christian Century 96(1979): 1125.

------., ed. When God and Man Failed: Non-Jewish Views of the Holocaust. New York: Macmillan, 1981.

Carmell, Aryeh., and Domb, Cyril., eds. Challenge: Torah View on Science and Its Problems. 2d rev. ed. Jerusalem: Feldheim, 1978.

Cavalieri, Liebe F. "Genetic Engineering: Who Decides What?" Baltimore Sun, 16 January 1983, p. K3.

Cobb, John B., ed. The Theology of Altizer: Critique and Response. Philadelphia: Westminister, 1970. The title of this work refers to Thomas J.J. Altizer, a theologian who questioned belief in the gracious and providential love of G-d after Auschwitz.

Cohen, Arthur A. The Myth of the Judeo-Christian Tradition and Other Dissenting Essays. New York: Schocken, 1971.

------. The Tremendum: A Theological Interpretation of the Holocaust. New York: Crossroad NY, 1981.

Cohn, Haim. The Trial and Death of Jesus. New York: Ktav, 1977.

Cohn, Norman. "The Myth of the Jewish World-Conspiracy: A Case Study in Collective Psychopathology." Commentary 41(1966): 35-42.

Comstock, W. Richard et al., eds. Religion and Man: An Introduction. New York: Har-Row, 1971.

Conway, John S. "Antisemitism and the Conflict in the Churches Since 1945." Christian Jewish Relations 16(1983): 21-37.

Crausnick, Helmut and Broszat, Martin. *The Anatomy of the SS State*. Translated by Dorothy Long and Marian Jackson. London: Paladin, 1973.

    Part One: Persecution of Jews;
    Part Two: The Concentration Camps.

Crozier, Michel. *The Bureaucratic Phenomenon*. Chicago: U of Chicago Pr, 1964.

------. *The Stalled Society*. New York: Viking Pr. 1973.

Davies, Alan T. *Anti-Semitism and the Christian Mind: The Crisis of Conscience after Auschwitz*. New York: Herder, 1969.

------. "Response to Irving Greenberg." In *Auschwitz: Beginning of a New Era?: Reflections on the Holocaust* edited by Eva Marie Fleischner, pp. 57-64. New York: Ktav, 1977.

------., ed. *Antisemitism and the Foundations of Christianity*. New York: Paulist Pr, 1979.

Dawidowicz, Lucy S. "The Holocaust Was Unique in Intent, Scope, and Effect." *Center Magazine* 14(1981): 56-64.

------. "Lies About the Holocaust." *Commentary* 70(1980): 31-37.

------. *The War Against the Jews 1933-1945*. New York: Bantam, 1978.

De Saint-Exupery, Antoine. *The Little Prince*. Translated by Katherine Woods. New York: Harcourt, Brace and World, 1943.

De Unamuno, Miguel. *The Tragic Sense of Life in Man and Nations*. Translated by Anthony Harrigan. Princeton: Princeton U Pr, 1970.

    Miguel de Unamuno (1864-1936) was a Spanish existential philosopher, and poet.

Des Pres, Terrence. *The Survivor: An Anatomy of Life in the Death Camps*. New York: Oxford U Pr, 1976.

Dong, Stella. "Study Criticizes Coverage of the Holocaust by 43 Current History Textbooks." Publishers Weekly 216(1979): 296.

Donin, Hayim Halevy. To Be a Jew: A Guide to Jewish Observance in Contemporary Life. New York: Basic, 1972.

------. To Raise a Jewish Child: A Guide for Parents. New York: Basic, 1977.

Dorff, Elliot N. "God and the Holocaust." Judaism 26(1977): 27-34.

Durang, Christopher. Sister Mary Ignatius Explains It All for You and The Actor's Nightmare. New York: Dramatists Play, 1982.

Eckardt, A. Roy. "Christians and Jews: Along a Theological Frontier." Encounter 40(1979): 89-127.

------. Elder and Younger Brother: The Encounter of Jews and Christians. New York: Scribner, 1967.

------. "Is the Holocaust Unique?," Worldview 17(1974): 31-35.

------. "The Recantation of the Covenant?" In Confronting the Holocaust, edited by Irving Greenberg and Alvin H. Rosenfeld, pp. 159-68. Bloomington, Ind.: Ind U Pr, 1978.

------. Your People, My People: The Meeting of Jews and Christians. New York: Quadrangle, 1974.

Eckardt, A. Roy., and Eckardt, Alice L. Long Night's Journey into Day: Life and Faith after the Holocaust. Detroit: Wayne St U Pr, 1982.

Eckardt, Alice L. "The Holocaust: Christian and Jewish Response." Journal of the American Academy of Religion 42(1974): 453-69.

Eckardt, Alice L., and Eckardt, A. Roy. "Studying the Holocaust's Impact Today: Some Dilemmas of Language and Method." Judaism 27(1978): 222-32.

Eckman, Lester Samuel. The History of the Musar Movement 1840-1945. New York: Shengold, 1975.

Eliach, Yaffa. "The Holocaust as Obligation and Excuse." *Center for Holocaust Studies Newsletter* 2(1980): 5,9.

Eliot, Gil. *Twentieth Century Book of the Dead*. New York: Scribner, 1972.

Epstein, Isodore. *Judaism: A Historical Presentation*. Baltimore, Penguin, 1966.

Everett, Robert A. "The Impact of the Holocaust on Christian Theology." *Christian Jewish Relations* 15(1982): 3-11.

Reverend Everett is pastor of Emanuel United Church of Christ in Irvington, New Jersey. His article is an excellent review of what the Christian agenda should be vis-a-vis Judaism.

Fackenheim, Emil L. "Jewish Faith and the Holocaust: A Fragment." *Commentary* 46(1968): 30-36.

------. *The Jewish Return into History: Reflections in the Age of Auschwitz and a New Jerusalem*. New York: Schocken, 1978.

------. "The People Israel Lives." *Christian Century* 87(1970): 563-68.

------. *To Mend the World: Foundations of Future Jewish Thought*. New York: Schocken, 1982.

Fast, Howard. *The Jews: Story of a People*. New York: Dell, 1978.

Feingold, Henry L. "Who Shall Bear Guilt for the Holocaust: The Human Dilemma." *American Jewish History* 68(1979): 261-82.

Dr. Feingold is professor of history at the Graduate Center of the City University of New York (CUNY) and Baruch College in New York.

Ferencz, Benjamin B. *Less Than Slaves: Jewish Forced Labor and the Quest for Compensation*. Cambridge: Harvard U. Pr, 1978.

Feyerabend, Paul K. *Against Method: Outline of an Anarchistic Theory of Knowledge*. London: NLB, 1975.

Paul Feyerabend received his Ph.D. from the University of Vienna and is now a professor of philosophy. He has published numerous articles on philosophy, science, and the philosophy of science.

------. Science in a Free Society. London: NLB, 1978.

Fischer, John. "God after the Holocaust: An Attempted Reconciliation." Judaism 32(1983): 309.20.

Fleischner, Eva Marie. "The Christian and the Holocaust." Journal of Ecumenical Studies 7(1970): 331-33.

------. "The Crucial Importance of the Holocaust for Christians." Engage/Social Action, December 1976, pp. 26-33.

------., ed. Auschwitz: Beginning of a New Era?: Reflections on the Holocaust. New York: Ktav, 1977.

Forrester, Jay W. "Churches at the Transition Between Growth and World Equilibrium." In Toward Global Equilibrium: Collected Papers, edited by Dennis L. Meadows and Donella H. Meadows, pp. 337-53. Cambridge, Mass.: Wright-Allen Pr, 1973.

Dr. Jay W. Forrester is professor of management at MIT and director of the System Dynamics Group in the Alfred P. Sloan School of Management at MIT.

The editor Dennis Meadows is professor of engineering and of business at Dartmouth College in Hanover, New Hampshire. He received his doctcrate in system dynamics from MIT. Dr. Meadows is director of the Phase One Study for the Club of Rome's Project on the Predicament of Mankind.

Donella Meadows is professor of Environmental Studies at Dartmouth. She received her doctorate in biophysics from Harvard.

Frey, Nancy R. "My Road to Judaism." Jewish Spectator 47(1982): 50-52.

Frey, Robert S. "Issues in Post-Holocaust Christian Theology." Dialog: A Journal of Theology 22(1983): 227-35.

Friedlander, Henry. "Toward a Methodology of Teaching about the Holocaust." Teachers College Record 80(1979): 519-42.

Friedlander, Henry., and Milton, Sybil. eds. The Holocaust: Ideology, Bureaucracy, and Genocide. Millwood, N.Y.: Kraus Intl, 1980.

> Dr. Friedlander teaches at the City College of New York. Dr. Milton is a respected archivist. This book is a collection of the scholarly papers delivered at the 1978 Holocaust conference held in San Jose, California.

Friedman, Mosheh Y'chiail. "Thoughts on the Nature of Man." Jewish Observer 16(1983): 6-9.

> Rabbi Friedman is director of the Torah Umesorah Counter-Force Program which provides counseling and therapeutic services to Yeshiva students and their families in New York City.

Fryshman, Bernard. "Computer Teaching in the Yeshiva: Processing the Data, Programming the Risks." Jewish Observer 16(1983): 14-16.

Gilbert, Martin. The Holocaust: A Record of the Destruction of Jewish Life in Europe During the Dark Years of Nazi Rule. New York: Hill & Wang, 1978.

Goldstein, Robert Justin. "The FBI's Forty-Year Plot." Nation 227(1978): 10-15.

> Dr. Goldstein teaches political science at Oakland University in Rochester, Michigan.

Gomer, Robert; Powell, John W.; and Röling, Bert V.A. "Japan's Biological Weapons: 1930-1945." Bulletin of the Atomic Scientists 37(1981): 43-53.

> Dr. Gomer is professor of chemistry at the University of Chicago. John W. Powell was born in China and educated in both China and the United States. During World War II, he

was an editor with the U.S. Office of War Information. From 1945 to 1953, Powell edited the China Weekly Review. Bert V.A. Röling was one of the judges in the International Military Tribunal for the Far East.

Greenberg, Blu. "Report of a Jewish Teacher." Ecumenist 12(1974): 84-86.

Greenberg, Irving. "Cloud of Smoke, Pillar of Fire: Judaism, Christianity and Modernity after the Holocaust." In Auschwitz: Beginning of a New Era?: Reflections on the Holocaust, edited by Eva Marie Fleischner, pp. 7-55, New York: Ktav, 1977.

------. "Judaism and Christianity after the Holocaust." Journal of Ecumenical Studies 12(1975): 521-51.

Greenberg, Irving., and Rosenfeld, Alvin H., eds. Confronting the Holocaust. Bloomington, Ind.: Ind U Pr, 1978.

Grunfeld, Isidor. The Sabbath: A Guide to Its Understanding and Observance. 4th ed. Jerusalem: Feldheim, 1981.

Hammer, Robert Alan. "The God of Suffering." Conservative Judaism 31(1976-77): 34-41.

Harrison, Everett F.; Bromiley, Geoffrey W.; and Henry, Carl F.H., eds. Baker's Dictionary of Theology. Grand Rapids, Mich.: Baker Bk, 1978.

Hauerwas, Stanley. "Jews and Christians Among the Nations: The Social Significance of the Holocaust." Cross Currents 31(1981): 15-34.

Heer, Friedrich. God's First Love: Christians and Jews Over 2000 Years. New York: Weybright and Talley, 1970.

Helmreich, William B. "Making the Awful Meaningful." Transaction Social Science and Modern Society 19(1982): 62-66.

Dr. Helmreich is professor of sociology and Judaic Studies at City College of New York and the City University Graduate Center. The article examines Orthodox Jewish response to the Holocaust.

Hick, John H. *Evil and the God of Love*. New York: Har-Row, 1966.

------., ed. *Classical and Contemporary Readings in Philosophy*. Englewood Cliffs, N.J.: Prentice-Hall, 1970.

Hilberg, Raul. *The Destruction of the European Jews*. New York: Har-Row, 1979.

------., ed. *Documents of Destruction*. Chicago: Quadrangle, 1971.

Hirsch, Samson Raphael., trans. *The Pentateuch*. 2d ed., rev. *Exodus*, vol. 2. Gateshead, N.Y.: Judaica Pr, 1982.

Höhne, Heinz. *The Order of the Deathshead: The Story of Hitler's SS*. Translated by Richard Barry. New York: Coward-McCann, 1970.

Horkheimer, Max. *Eclipse of Reason*. New York: Seabury, 1974.

Idinopulos, Thomas A. "Christianity and the Holocaust." *Cross Currents* 28(1978): 257-67.

------. "Humanistic Education in an Inhuman Age." *Cross Currents* 26(1977) 407-15.

Idinopulos, Thomas A., and Ward, Roy Bowen. "Is Christology Inherently Anti-Semitic?: A Critical Review of Rosemary Ruether's *Faith and Fratricide*." *Journal of the American Academy of Religion* 45(1977): 193-214.

Iggers, George G. "The Idea of Progress: A Critical Reassessment." *American Historical Review* 71(1965): 1-17.

Ilsar, Yehiel. "Theological Aspects of the Holocaust." *Encounter* 42(1981): 115-31.

Insko, Chester A., and Schopler, John. *Experimental Social Psychology*. New York: Acad Pr, 1973.

Isaac, Jules M. *The Teaching of Contempt*. New York: HR&W, 1964.

Johnson, Haynes. "Reagan's Eloquence Can't Mask Failure to Push Genocide Pact." Washington Post, 17 April 1983, p. A3.

Jonas, Hans. "Immortality and the Modern Temper." Harvard Theological Review 55(1962): 1-20.

Jones, James H. Bad Blood: The Tuskagee Syphilis Experiment. New York: Free Pr, 1981.

Jungk, Robert. "Altering the Director of Technology." Cross Currents 20(1970): 134-40.

Jungk, Robert., and Galtung, Johan., eds. Mankind 2000. London: Allen Unwin, 1970.

Future Research Monographs from the International Peace Research Institute in Oslo, Norway. (No. 1)

Kahane, Meir. Why Be Jewish?: Intermarriage, Assimilation, and Alienation. New York: Stein & Day, 1977.

Kaplan, Abraham. In Pursuit of Wisdom: The Scope of Philosophy. Beverly Hills: Glencoe Press, 1977.

Kaufman, Gordon D. "Nuclear Eschatology and the Study of Religion." Journal of the American Academy of Religion 51(1982): 3-14.

Kaufman makes the point, in discussing the threat of nuclear war, that changes in the historical situation demand changes in religious symbolism and frames of reference. Religion must be open to the historical process, changing to accommodate fundamental shifts in reality.

Kitov, Eliyahu. The Jew and His Home. 12th ed. Translated by Nathan Bulman. New York: Shengold, 1963.

Klein, Charlotte Lea. Anti-Judaism in Christian Theology. Philadelphia: Fortress, 1975.

Dr. Klein, a Roman Catholic, is a Tutor and Counsellor at the Open University in London. She is also a member of the team of the Study Centre for Jewish-Christian Relations in London.

Klein, Gerda Weissmann. *Promise of a New Spring: The Holocaust and Renewal.* Chappaqua, N.Y.: Rossel Bks, 1981.

>This book is intended for small children. The experience of the Jewish people in the Holocaust is presented in the motif of forest animals. There are several Holocaust-era photographs at the beginning of the book.

Kren, George M., and Rappoport, Leon. "Failures of Thought in Holocaust Interpretation." Mimeographed.

Kren, George M., and Rappoport, Leon. *The Holocaust and the Crisis of Human Behavior.* New York: Holmes & Meier, 1980.

Landes, David S. *The Unbound Prometheus: Technological Change and Industrial Development in Western Europe from 1750 to the Present.* Cambridge: Cambridge Univ. Press, 1969.

Lederberg, Joshua. "Orthobiosis: The Perfection of Man." In *The Place of Value in a World of Facts*, edited by Arne Tiselius and Sam Nilsson, pp. 29-58. Stockholm: Almqvist & Wiksell, 1970.

Lelyveld, Arthur J. *Atheism is Dead: A Jewish Response to Radical Theology.* Cleveland: World Publishing, 1968.

>Arthur Joseph Lelyveld (1913-) is a U.S. Reform rabbi and community leader.

Lifton, Robert Jay. "Medicalized Killing in Auschwitz." *Psychiatry* 45(1982): 283-97.

>Robert Lifton, M.D., is Foundations Fund Research Professor of Psychiatry at the Yale University School of Medicine.

Lincoln, Timothy Dwight. "Two Philosophies of Jewish History after the Holocaust." *Judaism* 25(1976): 150-57.

Littell, Franklin H. "Christendom, Holocaust, and Israel: The Importance for Christians of Recent Major Events in Jewish History." *Journal of Ecumenical Studies* 10(1973): 483-97.

------. The Crucifixion of the Jews. New York: Har-Row, 1975.

------. "A Report on Historical 'Revisionism'." Mimeographed. Philadelphia: National Institute on the Holocaust, 1981.

Littell, Franklin H., and Locke, Hubert G., eds. The German Church Struggle and the Holocaust. Detroit: Wayne St U Pr, 1974.

Löwith, Karl. Meaning in History: The Theological Implications of the Philosophy of History. Chicago: U of Chicago Pr, 1949.

Marcuse, Herbert. One Dimensional Man: Studies in the Ideology of Advanced Industrial Society. Boston: Beacon Pr. 1964.

Margolis, Max L., and Marx, Alexander. A History of the Jewish People. New York: Atheneum, 1978.

Maybaum, Ignaz. The Face of God after Auschwitz. Amsterdam: Polak and Van Gennup, 1965.

McCloskey, H.J.G. "God and Evil." In God and Evil, edited by Nelson Pike, pp. 61-84. Englewood Cliffs, N.J.: Prentice-Hall, 1964.

McEvoy, Donald W. A Christian Service of Holocaust Remembrance -- Yom HaShoah --. New York: National Conference of Christians and Jews, 1979.

McGarry, Michael B. Christology after Auschwitz. New York: Paulist Pr, 1977.

Meadows, Dennis L., and Meadows, Donella H., eds. Toward Global Equilibrium: Collected Papers. Cambridge, Mass.: Wright-Allen Pr, 1973.

Means, Richard L. The Ethical Imperative: The Crisis in American Values. Garden City, N.Y.: Anch. 1970

Milton, Mimsi. "Christians in the Galilee." Baltimore Jewish Times, 17 June 1983, pp. 62-64.

This article discusses the Christian agricultural settlement in Israel called Nes Ammim. The Christian inhabitants of this moshav settlement hope to atone for and redress the long history of Christian anti-Semitism through "lived solidarity with Israel". Living in a Jewish cultural context has helped many members of Nes Ammim to better understand and empathize with Jewish problems, social practices, and perspectives.

Mohr, Charles. "1941 Cables Boasted of Japanese-American Spying." New York Times, 22 May 1983, p. 18.

Moltmann, Jürgen. The Crucified God: The Cross of Christ as the Foundation and Criticism of Christian Theology. New York: Har-Row, 1974.

Monod, Jacques. "On Values in the Age of Science." In The Place of Value in a World of Facts, edited by Arne Tiselius and Sam Nilsson, pp. 19-27. Stockholm: Almqvist & Wiksell, 1970

Morse, Arthur D. While Six Million Died: A Chronicle of American Apathy. New York: Random, 1968.

"The Nazis' Forgotten Victims." Time, 19 November 1979, p. 58.

Nietzsche, Friedrich. Beyond Good and Evil: Prelude to a Philosophy of the Future. Translated by Walter Kaufman. New York: Random, 1966.

Novak, Michael. "The Family Is the Future." Readers Digest March 1978, pp. 110-13.

Nyiszli, Miklos. Auschwitz: A Doctor's Eyewitness Account. Translated by Tibere Kremer and Richard Seaver. Greenwich, Conn.: Fawcett, 1960.

Olson, Bernhard E. Faith and Prejudice. New Haven, Conn.: Yale U Pr, 1963.

Parkes, James William. The Conflict of the Church and the Synagogue: A Study in the Origins of Anti-Semitism. New York: Meridian Books, 1961.

The Reverend James Parkes was born in England and educated at Elizabeth College and Oxford. He became involved with contemporary anti-Semitism and Judaism when he was in Geneva, Switzerland as a member of the International Student Service. He has written extensively on these topics.

Pawlikowski, John T. The Challenge of the Holocaust for Christian Theology. New York: ADL, 1978.

------. Christ in the Light of the Christian Jewish Dialogue. New York: Paulist Pr, 1982.

------. "Church-State Relations: A Contemporary Catholic Perspective." Mimeographed. 1983.

This paper contains remarks which were originally presented to the Raleigh Summer Forum.

------. "The Holocaust as Rational Event." Reconstructionist 40(1974): 7-14.

------. "The Holocaust: Its Implications for the Church and Society Problematic." Encounter 42(1981): 143-54.

Peck, Abraham J., ed. Jews and Christians after the Holocaust. Philadelphia: Fortress, 1982.

Pfisterer, Rudolf. "Judaism in the Preaching and Teaching of the Church." Lutheran World 11(1964): 311-25.

Potok, Chaim. The Chosen. Greenwich, Conn.: Fawcett, 1967.

Rassinier, Paul. Debunking the Genocide Myth: A Study of the Nazi Concentration Camps and the Alleged Extermination of European Jewry. Translated by Adam Robbins. Los Angeles: Noontide, 1978.

This example of pseudo-revisionist literature is given an aura of credibility because the author is Jewish and evidently was an inmate at Auschwitz.

Rosenberg, Alan. "The Philosophical Implications of the Holocaust." In Perspectives on the Holocaust, edited by Randolph L. Braham, pp. 1-18. Boston: Kluwer-Nijhoff, 1983.

Alan Rosenberg is a lecturer in the Department of Philosophy at Queens College of CUNY.

Rubenstein, Richard L. After Auschwitz: Radical Theology and Contemporary Judaism. Indianapolis: Bobbs, 1978.

> This book is in its tenth printing.

------. The Age of Triage: Fear and Hope in an Overcrowded World. Boston: Beacon Pr, 1983.

------. The Cunning of History: The Holocaust and the American Future. New York: Har-Row, 1978.

------. "Some Perspectives on Religious Faith after Auschwitz." In The German Church Struggle and the Holocaust, edited by Franklin H. Littell and Hubert G. Locke, pp. 256-68. Detroit: Wayne St U Pr, 1974.

Ruether, Rosemary. Faith and Fratricide: The Theological Roots of Anti-Semitism. New York: Seabury, 1974

Russell, Bertrand. Authority and the Individual. Boston: Beacon Pr, 1960.

> Lord Russell (1872-1970) was an English philosopher, mathematician, author, and pacifist. He won a Nobel Prize in literature in 1950.

------. Why I am Not a Christian, and Other Essays on Religion and Related Subjects. Edited by Paul Edwards. New York: S & S, 1957.

Sandholtz, W.A. "Nuclear Disarmament." Chemical and Engineering News 61(1983): 3.

Scherman, Nosson., and Zlotowitz, Meir., eds. The Megillah/The Book of Esther. New York: Mesorah Pubns, 1981.

> This work is part of the ArtScroll Tanach Series.

Schiller, Mayer. The Road Back: A Discovery of Judaism Without Embellishment. 2d rev. ed. New York: Felheim, 1981.

Schwartz, Michael. "Are Christians Responsible?" National Review 32(1980): 956-58. Mr. Schwartz is executive director of the Catholic League for Religious and Civil Rights.

Schwartz-Bart, Andre. The Last of the Just. Translated by Stephen Becker. New York: Atheneum, 1960. (First American edition). The French title of this book is Le dernier des justes.

Seaborg, Glenn. "Science, Technology, and the Citizen." In The Place of Value in a World of Facts, edited by Arne Tiselius and Sam Nilsson, pp. 207-20. Stockholm: Almqvist & Wiksell, 1970.

Sereny, Gitta. Into That Darkness: From Mercy Killing to Mass Murder. New York: McGraw, 1974.

Shafran, Avi. Jewthink II: The Beauty of Antisemitism and Other Notes. Santa Barbara: Grapevine Press, 1981.

Sherman, Franklin. "Speaking of God after Auschwitz." Worldview 17(1974): 26-30.

Sherwin, Byron L., and Ament, Susan G., eds. Encountering the Holocaust: An Interdisciplinary Survey. Chicago: Impact Pr IL, 1979.

Silverman, David Wolf. "The Holocaust: A Living Force." Conservative Judaism 31(1976-77): 21-25.

Simon, Ulrich E. A Theology of Auschwitz. London: Victor Gollanz, 1967.

Skolimowski, Henryk. "The Scientific World View and the Illusions of Progress." Social Research 41(1974): 52-82.

Smith, Bradley F. Reaching Judgment at Nuremberg. New York: NAL, 1977.

Smith, Elwyn A. "The Christian Meaning of the Holocaust." Journal of Ecumenical Studies 6(1969): 22.

Smith, Huston. "Technology and Human Values: This American Moment." In Human Values and Advancing Technology, edited by Cameron Hall. New York: Friendship Pr, 1967.

Snell, Bradford C. "GM and the Nazis." Ramparts 12(1974): 15-16.

In 1974, Bradford Snell was assistant counsel to the Senate Monopoly and Anti-Trust Committee.

Sofer, Barbara. "Who Is a Convert?" Israel Scene 3(1982): 13-18.

Solzhenitsyn, Aleksandr. The Gulag Archipelago, 1918-1956: An Experiment in Literacy Investigation. 2 vols. Translated by Thomas P. Whitney. New York: Har-Row, 1974-75.

Staeglich, Wilhelm. The Auschwitz Myth. Tübingen, Germany: Grabert Publishing, 1979.

This is another example of pseudo-revisionist work.

Steckel, Charles W. "God and the Holocaust." Judaism 20(1971): 279-85.

Steiner, George. Language and Silence: Essays on Language, Literature, and the Inhuman. New York: Atheneum, 1967.

Steiner, Jean-Francois. Treblinka. New York: NAL, 1979.

Stern, Chaim. ed. Gates of Prayer: The New Union Prayerbook. New York: Central Conf, 1975.

Strassfeld, Sharon., and Strassfeld, Michael., eds. The Second Jewish Catalog. Philadelphia: JPS, 1976.

See particularly the chapter entitled "Teaching the Holocaust to Children," pp. 216-32. This chapter includes a teaching syllabus and bibliographical information which corresponds to that syllabus.

Strober, Gerald S. Portrait of the Elder Brother: Jews and Judaism in Protestant Teaching Materials. New York: National Conference of Christians and Jews, 1972.

Talmadge, Frank E. "Christian Theology and the Holocaust." Commentary 60(1975): 72-75.

This article reviews the work of Franklin H. Littell, Rosemary Ruether, and A. Roy Eckardt.

"38 Japanese-Americans to Get Compensation." New York Times, 15 May 1983, p. 18.

Thompson, Warren K.A. "Ranier C. Baum, The Holocaust and the German Elite: Genocide and National Suicide in Germany, 1871-1945." Business and Professional Ethics Journal 2(1982): 85-89.

Tiefel, Hans O. "Holocaust Interpretations and Religious Assumptions." Judaism 25(1976): 135-49.

Tillion, Germaine. Ravensbrück: An Eyewitness Account of a Women's Concentration Camp. Translated by Gerald Satterwhite. Garden City, N.Y.: Doubleday, 1975.

Tiselius, Arne., and Nilsson, Sam., eds. The Place of Value in a World of Facts. Stockholm: Almqvist & Wiksell, 1970.

Proceedings of the Fourteenth Nobel Symposium held in Stockholm, 15-20 September 1969.

United Methodist Reporter for Eastern Pennsylvania, 16 February 1979.

Van Buren, Paul M. Discerning the Way: A Theology of the Jewish-Christian Reality. New York: Seabury, 1980.

Walker, Williston. A History of the Christian Church. 3rd ed. New York: Charles Scribner's Sons, 1970.

Waskow, Arthur I. "Looking Forward: 1999." In Mankind 2000, edited by Robert Jungk and Johan Galtung, pp. 78-98. London: Allen Unwin, 1970.

White, Peter T. "Kampuchea Wakens from a Nightmare." National Geographic, May 1982, pp. 590-622.

Wiesel, Elie. Foreword to A Christian Response to the Holocaust, by Harry James Cargas. Denver: Stonehenge, 1981.

------. "Art and Culture after the Holocaust." In Auschwitz: Beginning of a New Era?: Reflections on the Holocaust, edited by Eva Marie Fleischner, pp. 403-415. New York: Ktav, 1977.

------. Night. New York: Avon, 1969.

Wiesenthal, Simon. Max and Helen. Translated by Catherine Hutter. New York: William Morrow, 1982.

Wilhelm, Anthony J. Christ Among Us: A Modern Presentation of the Catholic Faith. New York: Paulist Pr, 1973.

Will, George F. "The Threat to the Self." Baltimore Sun, 24 April 1983, p. K7.

Willis, Robert E. "Auschwitz and the Nurturing of Conscience." Religion in Life 12(1975): 432-47.

------. "Christian Theology after Auschwitz." Journal of Ecumenical Studies 12(1975): 493-519.

------. "Confessing God after Auschwitz: A Challenge for Christianity." Cross Currents 28(1978): 269-87.

Wolpin, Nisson. "The Case of the Non-Conserving Conservatives." Jewish Observer 16(1983): 4-9.

Woodward, Kenneth L., and Salholtz, Eloise. "Debate Over the Holocaust." Newsweek 10 March 1980, p. 97.

Wouk, Herman. This Is My God: The Jewish Way of Life. New York: Pocket Books, 1973.

Wykes, Alan. Himmler. New York: Ballantine Books, 1972. This book is number 14 in Ballantine's Illustrated History of the Violent Century.

Wyschogrod, Michael. "Faith and the Holocaust: A Review Essay of Emil Fackenheim's God's Presence in History." Judaism 20(1971): 286-94.

Zahn, Gordon C. "Catholic Responses to the Holocaust." Thought 56(1981): 153-62.

ABOUT THE AUTHORS

NANCY THOMPSON-FREY holds a Bachelor of Arts degree (with honors) from Lebanon Valley College in Annville, PA. Her prior publications are: "My Road to Judaism" in the Jewish Spectator (Summer, 1982) and "The Holocaust, Christianity, and Personal Response" in Christian-Jewish Relations (December, 1984 with Robert S. Frey). Ms. Thompson-Frey works as a housecounselor with mentally handicapped adults in Columbia, Maryland.

ROBERT SEITZ FREY holds a Bachelor of Science degree (with honors) from Lebanon Valley College in Annville, PA. He is actively pursuing a master of arts degree in modern Jewish history at Baltimore Hebrew College. Mr. Frey's prior publications are: "Issues in Post-Holocaust Christian Theology" in Dialog: A Journal of Theology (Summer, 1983) and "The Holocaust, Christianity, and Personal Response" in Christian-Jewish Relations (December, 1984 with Nancy Thompson-Frey).

Mr. Frey has lectured on the Holocaust at various Pennsylvania and Maryland colleges, universities, and Christian seminaries. He works as an information scientist in Baltimore, Maryland.